Taking Children

Richard Hubbard is available on a national and international basis to lead seminars on the topics covered in this book. You can write to him at the following address:

Richard Hubbard
PO Box 198
Littlehampton
West Sussex
BN17 6SP
England

For details of praise party cassettes, songbook and Rich's Powerpoint product range, please enclose a stamped addressed envelope.

Richard Hubbard

Taking Children Seriously

*Developing a children's ministry
in your church*

With a Foreword by
Ishmael

Marshall Pickering
An Imprint of HarperCollins Publishers

First published in Great Britain in 1991 by Marshall Pickering

Marshall Pickering is an imprint of
HarperCollins Religious,
part of HarperCollins Publishers
77–85 Fulham Palace Road, London W6 8JB

Typeset by Medcalf Type Ltd, Bicester, Oxon
Printed and bound in Great Britain by
HarperCollins Manufacturing, Glasgow

Contents

Foreword

For centuries many churches have looked upon children as unimportant, time-wasting little nuisances, who need to be contained until they reach teenage years. The pattern then follows, that the "unspiritual", worldly teens will wander off for a few years to find themselves amidst major traumas and backsliding. Hopefully at some stage, they reach the "settling down years". This usually involves marriage, children and, for a few, the re-attendance of church because history has told them that was the proper way to spend Sunday mornings.

Finally, as the next generation of children grows up and continues the cycle, our unimportant little time-wasting nuisances of yesteryear have now reached the age of fifty or sixty and, we are informed, "stood the test of time". This tiny remnant is accepted as being mature with a spiritual capacity which qualifies them to have church responsibilities and hopefully a ministry from God which all the younger ones should appreciate and support. So . . . from thousands of children, we end up with less than a handful of leaders.

Am I exaggerating the issue? I hope so, but from what I have seen as I have visited many hundreds of churches over the past twenty years I fear for many it contains more than an element of truth.

But the good news is that "the times they are a-changing". At least people are beginning to wake up to the fact that children are as much of God's plan as Archbishops and Apostles. Once saved they need good teaching and training, they are not only a vital part of our Church today but they are our leaders of tomorrow, and I mean tomorrow, not in fifty years' time.

The time has come when men and women of God will be active in bringing the hearts of the fathers back to their children, and helping the Church to see that they are a family, and each member of that family regardless of age needs to be respected, loved, grounded in scripture, then released to fulfil the ministry that God has prepared for them.

How we move from where we are to implement this will be a mammoth step for some, but it's a step we will have to take if we want to keep up with where the Spirit of God is moving us.

But . . . we cannot expect to pass this on to our children, if we adults have not got excited about the vision.

I believe this book will help to give you that vision.

Richard Hubbard is not subtle, I don't think that he knows what the word means. He's a man who loves his Lord, loves the Church and loves children, and he's a man committed to the cause of seeing children not just saved, but released into all that God has for them.

This book does not contain waffle and niceties. From page one it jumps on us, hammers us, turns our heads in a new direction, screaming out at us to open our eyes. In fact it tries every possible way to shake us out of a rut which has ended up being a grave for so many of our children.

We may like it or hate it, agree or disagree with it, but I promise that this book is vital reading, not just for the sake of the children, but for the sake of our present, our future and most of all for the Kingdom of God.

ISHMAEL
31st January 1991

Chapter 1

Kids in the Kingdom

After a six hour drive we were glad to arrive. We had been very careful to follow the directions given on the map and had now arrived at the right town. It was a good start!

After negotiating various bends and junctions we eventually arrived in an area that could have come straight out of Coronation Street. Here we found the organisers of the children's meetings we were to lead that week. They took us to the church.

When we arrived the large double doors were unlocked and flung open to reveal. . .the smallest church building I had ever seen! It was marginally bigger than an average front room. In spite of its somewhat underwhelming proportions it was fully equipped with organ, pipes, polished communion table, embroidered collection bags— the whole works.

The problem was: where would we put our PA system? Did we even need it? What about the overhead projector? Where would we put the stage lights? All these and other interesting questions had me feeling unusually depressed! One of the lads had climbed into the pulpit at the front and was leaning out very dangerously in a frantic effort to find somewhere for the OHP screen. I was most concerned about this as it seemed to me that the message contained on the neat overhanging pulpit cloth, "He is risen", was just about to be overtaken by events!

The time came for the first session to start. We had already turned the volume controls down to virtually zero and were ready for the vast armies of high-spirited children we expected.

1

The meeting was due to start at 6.00pm. By 6.05pm there was not a single person in the church. A slow trickle brought in a grand total of eighteen children to this special regional extravaganza. In the event it was almost a capacity crowd. At least we were able to joke that another half dozen would have meant turning people away!

The opening session was very difficult. No one would sing. In spite of jokes, funny faces, over-the-top stupidity (my contribution), everyone just sat there on the fixed pews looking at us! Then during one of the songs one of the boys got up holding his ears and ran out of the church. Things can only get better, I thought.

But as the week wore on the children gradually warmed up. In the end they got so excited in their praise and worship they ended up dancing on the pews!

Looking around the church building later I came upon the Sunday school classroom. On the door was the well known picture of Jesus outside the door of a person's heart, based on Revelation 3:20. The picture was old, faded and unattractive. Inside was the musty smell of old hymn-books quietly rotting in a corner. On the walls were various colourings which had obviously been done by the children a long time ago. Other pictures showed Jesus in old-fashioned clothes from the Middle East. In one corner was a flannelgraph and a fuzzy-felt board. The whole image was low-key and dated.

I stood outside the church in the warm evening air and thought to myself, "Surely our children deserve more than this?" My life in a funny sort of a way would never be quite the same again. I determined that for as long as my ministry involved children and families, I would work hard to see change within the Kingdom of God in the way we deal with our children and young people.

Rise and Shine
Over the past twenty-five years or so we have seen the

start of a spiritual awakening in Britain. Naturally there is still a long way to go but equally the church has come quite a long way, at least in some circles. As has been well stated elsewhere, we have come through an era of personal renewal, are coming through an era of corporate restoration and are moving on towards national revival. I believe this fully and am very excited about it! A large part of my own ministry nowadays is to be a prophetic voice to the Church in our generation to see it shaping up for revival.

In spite of the renewal we have experienced, it seems to me that our children's work is still being done very much as it was before. Renewal has largely failed to touch our children's and young people's ministry in any real way. One of the things I am convinced is firmly on God's agenda for the Church in the 'nineties is that we recognise this and see the renewal we are expecting amongst adults taught to and experienced by our children. If taken on board seriously, this will radically affect the shape of the Church in the nation.

The question is this: Are we prepared to respond to what God is saying and make radical changes to the structure of our churches and fellowships?

Many will want the benefits but will not be prepared for the cost of change. It will be a costly business. Inevitably there will be those who will decry radical changes. But it is my prayer that many church leaders will grasp the nettle firmly and bring about the change that we so desperately need in the Church of the 'nineties.

Attitudes

As a general rule children's ministry in our churches has an abysmally low profile. The "real" church is perceived to be where the adults are. Their activities are the real business of the Church. Children should be seen and not heard, or better still not even seen at all! Often adults can hardly wait until it is Sunday school time so that they can get rid of the children. Under a thin veneer of being all family together and of the children belonging with us in the church, there lurks the reality that children are not altogether welcome.

Anyone in any doubt about this should read the latest balance sheet of their own church (for a little light reading at bedtime). I must confess to disliking so-called business meetings where we talk about the boiler, the colour of the wallpaper—everything in fact except the *real* business of the Kingdom. However, looking at the figures will prove very interesting. How much has been spent on the children as a percentage of what has been spent on the adults? Do our children have the best equipment, ministry resources and people, or are all these hoarded for the adults? Have we invested in training and equipping people with real ability and anointing or has this been lavished on adults only?

At one church I visited in Wales I was setting up the equipment before the meeting while a few others were putting out the chairs. I overheard a lady tell her helpers to put the tatty chairs at the front as all the children and youth would be sitting there! In another church, I was attending to the call of nature in the meeting venue, an old hut where the toilet facilities were a little basic. There on the floor of the toilet in a dustbin liner were large pieces of card on which were written the words to children's songs used in the Sunday school.

Whilst it would not be fair to say that all churches have such a low view of their children, it is true that in most churches the whole ethos and image of children's ministry are in need of radical revamp.

Not only has children's work been given a low priority but the children themselves have a very raw deal inside the church. Many leaders might be embarrassed to realise that they probably do not even know the names of some

4

of the children, far less have any sort of friendship with them.

Furthermore we tend to regard our children as unevangelised pagans rather than as people with a capacity for real spiritual development. Time and time again I have seen people doing a children's talk competing to use an even better visual aid than the person last week. We get more and more sophisticated in our presentations so that we could write whole books on what to do with the inside of an old toilet roll! Yet for all this the basic message we are proclaiming is the same basic message. We constantly bombard our children with clever talks on what it means to become a Christian. Although this is extremely important we must also realise that we have a responsibility to take the children on from there into (or at least towards) spiritual maturity. If we do not do this our children will quickly grow up thinking that they know it all and that they have heard it all before. Those who have already given their lives to Jesus need more. Those who have not done so as yet get dulled to the cutting edge of the good news through overfamiliarity.

Children are not part of the Church of tomorrow. They are part of the Church today. They are not some kind of unrealised potential but they are with us now! They need to feel a part of us. Is it really any wonder that having been talked down to at a most basic level all their lives, they are off at the first opportunity as soon as they hit their teens? The miracle is that they are not off sooner.

All my yesterdays
In order to set the stage for all that follows in this book, it would probably be a good idea for me to introduce myself and explain something of my background and what has led me to work on a national basis with adults, children and the whole family.

My love for children stems from the fact that I am really

a big kid myself. Mind you, I have apparently been showing signs of growing up lately. My wife Lynda thinks that I must be approaching my teenage years now as I seem to be getting slightly rebellious—albeit a little later in life! Actually this is not quite true. I prefer to think of it as being prophetic rather than rebellious!

At the age of nine and a half, having been a Christian for about two years, I began to feel the call of God on my life to serve him when I grew up. It was following a visit by Billy Graham to London during which time I went to hear him preach at Earls Court. We went by coach. Everyone seems to go by coach when travelling to hear Billy Graham. I remember eating one of those brown bourbon biscuits on the way up to London—I was only allowed to have one as overindulgence was a sin!

The ministry of Billy Graham was quite an influence on me as a child and I am sure that God used it to shape my own call into Christian ministry. I used to sit in my bedroom and wonder how I would get to these major venues like Earls Court where I would be preaching. My bicycle was still a little big for me and in any case I had not really mastered the gears. London was quite a long way away—about twenty-two miles from where we then lived in Caterham, Surrey, but I figured that if the worst came to the worst someone would probably give me a lift!

Although my thinking was very much as a child, God was nevertheless beginning to work powerfully within my own little life and calling me to serve him. We must never look at childish ways and then conclude that God's work must always be done by mature grown-ups. We need to recognise the capacity children can have for a powerful awareness of God.

This really hit me rather more recently when I was running the children's celebration meetings at EuroFire. There we saw amazing things happening in all of our lives. Children —and leaders, too—were healed, children were filled with the Holy Spirit and began to speak in tongues and prophesy. It was all happening!

Yet I noticed that in spite of the very real presence of God, children who one minute would be praying for healing would the next minute be kicking each other! A little playful fight broke out just near someone who had been "slain in the Spirit" and was flat out on the floor! I learned this: kids will be kids! Let us not deny them opportunities for real spiritual growth just because they may not yet be fully developed in other areas. After all, are we as adults really all that different? Let us not deny them the opportunities to grow in all that God has for them even while they are still children.

I was brought up in the Open Brethren. Although as a family we did not attend all that regularly it seemed to get more regular as I got a little older. I remember one Sunday evening surprising everyone by deciding that I wanted to go to the gospel service. This was a surprise to my parents as we only used to go to the hall (later renamed chapel) in the mornings. These were the days when the church was something you went to rather than something you were a part of. The evening gospel service was the occasion when the gospel would be preached faithfully—to Christians. It was a lively occasion as a real piano was used to assist us in our music! The morning meetings were the more sombre times when the singing was unaccompanied by any form of musical instrument. The real reason I wanted to go that evening was because my Mum wanted to give me a spelling test in readiness for the real thing at school the next day. I knew that the game of Spiritual Blackmail would do the trick. After all, what Christian parent would say no to their child expressing an interest in going to church?

When I reached the grand old age of twelve I had a spiritual crisis. On the one hand I had had quite enough of Church, and yet on the other hand I had a real and genuine faith in God. I knew that my life belonged to Jesus but I just could not understand why Church seemed so miserable. "There must be something more to it than this," I thought, but I did not have a clue what it could be.

At this time things were getting pretty tough at school. I was telling all my friends about Jesus. This was partly because I really did want them to know, but it was also partly because I had been brought up with the idea that every keen Christian really ought to be an evangelist. Whatever the reasons for sharing my faith the results were clear. On one occasion I was held up on a football pitch (I have always hated football!) whilst others took it in turns to kick a ball at me simply because I was a Christian! On another occasion I suggested to one of the Big Boys in the school that a lad in my class who was a cripple could be healed by prayer. This Big Boy immediately went off into such a verbal frenzy at me that I was left quaking at the knees.

God has a wonderful way of providing exactly what is needed at exactly the right time. In all this I needed a spiritual wash-and-brush-up. When my parents had some new carpet fitted the man doing the fitting turned out to be a Christian. I just happened to be in the room—probably sensing that Mum would offer him a cup of tea and I might get one too—when I heard something that made my ears prick up. He was telling Mum that at his church so many people were becoming Christians and joining in that they had to tear down the old tin hut where they met and build a brand new purpose-built, fully equipped church.

My mouth fell open as I heard him tell of some of the miracles and healings that were taking place and of the young people's group that was bursting at the seams. I was beginning to think that Christian young people were extinct. I almost thought I had heard somewhere that they were not for today but went out with the Apostles! I was very interested to hear that Youth was not an endangered species. My insides wanted to burst with joy and expectation. Could this be what I was looking for?

I went along. It was a Pentecostal church (at that time) in Sutton. I could not believe it! The atmosphere was completely different. The people were happy. They also seemed very genuine and very warm. The worship went like a rocket rather than like a lead balloon. There were an electric guitar and drums but it was not the externals that attracted me. I could not have cared less if the worship was led on bagpipes—there was something *spiritually* different.

It was so good that I insisted that my English teacher came. It was one Friday afternoon and all eyes (including both of mine) were fixed on the clock in anticipation of the final bell. As we were finishing off I felt that I should ask him to come to the meeting on Sunday. I wrestled with the idea, thinking that it was not the done thing and this "feeling" might be just me rather than God. The bell went and before I knew what had happened I went down to the front and asked him. He said Yes. That Sunday he gave his life to Jesus. I was ecstatic!

I soon realised however that although I was a Christian just like anyone else in the church, they had something I knew I did not have but very much wanted. The "it" turned out to be a "he" as I learned for the first time about the Holy Spirit. I had heard practically nothing about the Holy Spirit in my upbringing. Doctrinally I knew he was part of the Godhead, but he meant very little in practical terms to me personally. I had assumed that the Holy Spirit was merely some kind of a Godly influence. After a lot of struggle I was filled with the Holy Spirit and realised I now had a personal relationship with two of the three members of the Trinity. It was to be a little while before I found out something about the fatherhood of God.

From there in 1974 I began to go to one or two naughty meetings on the side! I began to go as often as I could get there to a new fellowship which had recently been started in Kingston. I was only ever a fringe person but again God used the experience to show me as a very spotty youth of fifteen that there was even more to Kingdom living than I had experienced! I grew so much spiritually during that year and in one of these meetings did my first public ''preach''.

Moving away to West Sussex and to the coast I discovered a then-struggling little fellowship in Rustington which at that time was linked to the Baptist church in Littlehampton. The fellowship had been started in 1972 and at the time was a sort of cross between a Brethren assembly and a Pentecostal church. Being sixteen and mobile on my Yamaha FS1-E 50cc moped (which I rode as if it were a 500cc proper bike!) I began to attend regularly. My beautiful young girlfriend who had previously attended the Baptist church started coming along with me. Six years later we got married.

As is normal in fellowship life there were ups and downs but God was at work. The leaders were spiritual men with open hearts. They taught me a lot about commitment, personal vulnerability and dealing with hurts and issues of the past.

Apart from time out at university and six years of emigration to Cornwall we have been here ever since. The fellowship (now called Arun Christian Fellowship) has grown and developed, planted out one congregation so far (with more to follow) and developed links with Gerald Coates and the Pioneer team. Significantly there has been a great emphasis on the family and the place of children in the Church. This vision was later caught by a very good mate Ishmael who moved in six years after the fellowship started. Although there is no such thing as a perfect church I am very glad indeed to be a part of it.

One fact that I have learned from moving around is that children need to be securely based and rooted in at local church level. It is vital that the right environment is created to enable children to develop and to flourish spiritually. All of my nipping around here, there and everywhere in my early days was in many ways unhelpful. However all this was in the early days of the Spirit working in a corporate context and I was hungry! Nowadays thankfully there is so much more potential locally for families to be part of something that is working strategically for God.

Recent travels

I thank God that things are changing on the church scene. In the past I sometimes cringed when asked to lead certain kinds of children's meetings. Now my own involvement is shifting away from local church children's meetings and much more towards whole-family all-age celebration sessions and seminars. This change of emphasis has come about because it is so necessary to break down the adult-children barrier. Doing child-only meetings merely reinforces this barrier and does nothing to tear it down.

Recently I was invited to Southampton Community Church to take a large children's celebration meeting. Having done a seminar on the Saturday followed by another meeting in the evening, we were all ready for the children's session. The meeting was in a modern building which is part of the university. It was a thoroughly Christian but totally non-religious occasion. The large room was packed and the atmosphere brilliant. We were able not only to do some teaching but saw a significant number responding to the Lord and asking to be filled with the Holy Spirit. As these children were worshipping in tongues with their little hands in the air having had some turbo-praise and worship, I thought to myself, *"This* is much more what children's work inside the Kingdom is all about."

I have found that bookings do not have to be big to be beautiful. Numbers are unimportant. It is the attitude and expectation of the leaders that will make the difference, and the openness of the children. A small houseparty near Scarborough with about fifteen or so children turned out to be one of the best. Again lots of prayers of healing and

11

against all sorts of very real fears went on. Most were filled with the Holy Spirit by the end of the weekend and were learning to use the gifts of the Spirit. Something very similar happened recently at a weekend away near Exeter where most of the children were spoken to in some way and where many were again filled with the Holy Spirit.

The approach adopted in these sessions is, to me, much more what children's work is all about. When we compare them to the kind of meeting mentioned at the beginning of this chapter we can see that there is a fresh wind blowing. Praise God for those who have gone before and laid a foundation, but how we need a new generation of children's workers who are filled with the Holy Spirit and are great fun and yet whose communication skills match any well known contemporary preacher to adults.

Chapter 2

Back to the Bible

Once a person becomes a Christian he or she immediately becomes part of the worldwide family of God that goes to make up the Church. There is no period of unofficial probation to see if everything works out, there is an immediate adoption into the Kingdom of God.

When a child becomes a Christian it is no different. He or she immediately becomes part of the Church. We all know this, of course. But do we act as though we believe it?

It is often said within the Church that we must look after our children because they are some kind of potential for the future—part of the Church of tomorrow. Actually this is only partly true. If they have really given their lives to the Lord Jesus children are not merely part of the Church of tomorrow, they are actually part of the Church of today. All too often we view children as "potential" or as "tomorrow's Church" without really seeing that they are every bit a part of it now as we as adults are! In fact my experience leads me to believe that children are actually able to usher in tomorrow's Church today!

The Bible has a lot to say about children, young people and families. To really understand what it teaches may need a slightly broader approach to biblical teaching than is sometimes taken. The traditional way to find out God's perspective on a particular issue is to look up a few key words in a concordance and find all the references. For example, if we want a little teaching on faith we can look the word up and begin to build up a good picture of what the Bible teaches on the subject. However, when it comes to children and young people in the Church we need to understand that there are relatively few passages specifically and directly concerned with teaching in this area. We will not get very far using our concordance type of approach.

Another way to receive what the Bible teaches is to look not only at what is taught systematically but at the prevailing attitudes and understandings that are beneath the surface. If we search the pages of the Bible with our spiritual eyes trained to read between the lines as well as on them, we will find that there is an amazing amount of teaching throughout the whole of scripture. Of course it is important that our interpretation of scripture does not become purely subjective. Some people can make the Bible say whatever they want it to say. It is important therefore to recognise that one scripture must be read alongside other scripture so as to get the tenor of the whole Bible.

What follows is a selection of incidents from the Bible to give us a flavour of God's perspective on children and young people. It is not intended as an exhaustive list.

Joseph: the Prophetic Dreamer (Genesis 37–50)
Joseph was seventeen when God appeared to him in a dream and showed him that his older brothers would actually serve him.

Joseph was the youngest and appears to be the favourite. He was born to Jacob when he was getting on in years and had been given a special multi-coloured robe—a sort of rainbow jumper! His brothers hated him for this, and what made matters worse was that Joseph followed God. A number of incidents had not particularly endeared his brothers to him, such as the tales of their conduct out in the field which Joseph had carefully reported back to Dad.

Joseph's dream did nothing to heal the ever-widening rift between him and his brothers. In fact, it only made matters worse. It was a strange dream. In it Joseph and his brothers were tying up sheaves of wheat in the field when all of a sudden Joseph's stood up straight. The other sheaves formed a circle around it and bowed down to it. The interpretation was obvious and made the other brothers very angry.

It did not end there. Joseph had another dream This time he saw the sun, moon and eleven stars bowing down to him. Naturally his brothers were not too happy with this and when the dream was told to Jacob he too was a little cautious about it.

In spite of the opposition Joseph knew that God was speaking to him. He was only a young man. In our society he would have been only just old enough to drive a car yet God had given him a prophetic ministry. Whilst everyone else was trying to sift it all through reason and logic, the word of God throbbed inside him. Joseph was just the sort of guy that might be perceived to be a little dangerous by local church leaders!

What happened next was difficult to understand and seemed to go against the word he thought he had received. Joseph was thrown down into a pit, then sold to Midianite traders who took him to Egypt and sold him as a slave. Then he was flung into jail for allegedly interfering with Potiphar's wife, which was untrue. In jail he was forgotten even by the two people he had helped.

Years later he had again regained favour with Potiphar and became Prime Minister. During a famine in Israel when things became desperate, Jacob sent his sons to buy food from Egypt and Joseph's brothers came to him cap in hand without realising it was him. Joseph was then aged thirty-seven.

We need to understand that God will call some of our children and young people into ministry. Sometimes those with gifting seem like angry young men who at a stroke want to put everything right. Even Jacob was very dubious about his favourite son!

In all this we need to make room for emerging leadership

and give our young people room in the church to
manoeuvre.

Samuel: a Childhood Priest (1 Samuel 1–3)

This is one of my favourite Old Testament stories. It gets
me excited every time I read it! Samuel was a boy, an
ordinary boy, but this little chap had been given back to
the Lord by his mother Hannah even before he was born.
When he was very young, in fact as soon as he was on to
solids rather than milk, he was taken to the Temple to live
and to be trained up by the priest Eli. Samuel was little more
than a baby. He knew nothing about life, far less did he
have any kind of spiritual discernment at that time. But
God's hand was already on his little life.

As the boy grew Eli would have had to teach him everything, not just the spiritual bits of life but ordinary things
as well. I can just imagine Eli teaching him to drink from
a cup, and trying to potty-train him as well as teaching him
to pray! As time went on Eli was able to teach him more
and more about the God of Israel and encourage him to
listen to God for himself and to develop his own relationship
with the Lord.

We do not know exactly how Eli did the teaching. Part
of it like our present-day school work may have been by
systematic lessons, but much of it would have been simply
by example. As young Samuel looked at what Eli did in his
whole lifestyle, not just what he said with his mouth, he
would have learned a lot. Often with discipleship it is what
is caught rather than what is taught that is the most relevant.
Eli would have known this.

Every year Samuel would get a visit from his mother as
a special treat! In fact each year Hannah would bring Samuel
new clothes because he was growing all the time and last
year's clothing would be getting a little small. The clothes
that Hannah made were very special garments, ephods,
made of linen and worn only by priests. Even as a child

Samuel was beginning to perform a priestly function. He was becoming active in his own ministry.

As a child Samuel knew what it was to hear the voice of God. Naturally Eli had to help him along with this to start with, but once Samuel knew what it was all about God began to speak to him about some very important issues. In fact God even spoke to Samuel about things of profound importance and gave him the difficult job of foretelling judgment within Eli's own family. The prophetic ministry has never been easy.

In 1 Samuel 3:19–21 (Good News Bible) it says:

"As Samuel grew up the Lord was with him and made everything that Samuel said come true. So all the people of Israel from one end of the country to the other knew that Samuel was indeed a prophet of the Lord. The Lord continued to reveal himself at Shiloh where he had appeared to Samuel and had spoken to him."

Then the phrase that always amazes me:

"When Samuel spoke all Israel listened."

A child—but one who had begun to minister and who, as we know, later became a national spiritual leader.

The question for us is this: If Samuel were in our church today how would we treat him? Would we encourage him in his ministry or would we give him a colouring to do?

David the Giantkiller (1 Samuel 17)
David was the youngest brother of four sons of Jesse. David's brothers were all soldiers in the Israelite army. They had been trained up for battle. War with the Philistines seemed inevitable.

To David, the older brothers were real heroes. Imagine his delight when his Dad asked him to take a food parcel of bread to them with some cheese for the officers. Not only was it an incredible privilege but it was a chance to see the inside of a real army camp. He would be able to see his older brothers in action!

To make his visit even more exciting, the King happened to turn up while David was visiting. But during his visit David got caught up in a very tense situation. The giant from the Philistine camp over the valley on the opposite hill was breathing out threats. War seemed inevitable. And the stakes were high. Whichever nation lost would have to serve the other. This was not the place for a novice.

David was not given a warm welcome. His brothers told him to push off as the army camp was a place for real men, not youthful sightseers who were only capable of looking after a few sheep! But when the giant spoke, something in David's heart stirred. The Israelite army had been trying to cope with the crisis of not having a suitable man to fight with the Philistine giant. Despite the training, the equipment and the promised reward, no one was either capable or willing to fight.

Suddenly, right in front of the King, David blurted it out: "I'll do it—I'll fight!" Roars of laughter no doubt echoed in the valley between the two opposing forces. Despite the inevitable opposition and criticism that he was only a boy and far too young for this sort of thing, the King consented.

David was not a professional, he had no training, he could not even fit comfortably into the King's armour that was offered to him. All he had was a catapult, five stones—and God.

David's victory over the giant is well known. The secret of his strength was summed up in his own brief childlike address to the giant (1 Samuel 17:45):

> "You come against me with sword and spear and javelin,
> but I come against you in the name of the Lord Almighty,
> the God of the armies of Israel, whom you have defied."

David was a young person. What he did shaped the history of a nation. The account of his victory is one of the best known and best loved stories in the Bible. Would it have happened if David had been older? Can we realistically continue to talk down to children and young people who may actually end up achieving more than we do?

Elisha and the Lad (2 Kings 4:8–37)
The signs and wonders ministry of Elisha has a lot to teach us. The amazing thing as far as children and young people are concerned is that Elisha's powerful ministry was not reserved for the high and mighty but affected the lives of young people, too.

The rich woman from Shunem had all she wanted—except a child. She and her husband regularly provided Elisha with accommodation for the odd night whilst Elisha was busy ministering. In fact the spare room was made up ready and a bed, table and lamp had been installed for him. What a blessing that room must have been to Elisha. No wonder he was grateful. Elisha wanted to do something in return. When he discovered that the real desire of his hostess's heart was to have a child, he prayed and prophesied over her. In due course—in nine months, to be exact—she produced what to her was no doubt the best baby boy in all the world!

God used Elisha in a very real and down-to-earth way to meet a very real and down-to-earth need. It was not a great spiritual request. The lady simply wanted a baby and God heard her request.

But after several years disaster struck. The Shunamite woman thought the bottom had just fallen out of her world. The child was carried in from the field one morning where he had been helping Dad, complaining of a headache. A few hours later at noon the unthinkable happened. He died.

Imagine the thoughts going through the lady's mind. In desperation she laid the boy on his bed and sent for Elisha. We do not know exactly how old the child was but he was carried to his mother and was nursed on her lap until she died. Obviously he was still young. When Elisha arrived he stretched himself over the body, then got up for a walk round, then lay over the body again. The boy's body became warm He sneezed, then woke up!

It is amazing to think that so much scripture space is given to a very domestic, family scene. The miraculous was brought into the very ordinariness of the life of a child both in his conception and in his resuscitation.

Naaman's Girl (2 Kings 5)

The miracle of the healing of Naaman, the Syrian army chief, is well known. This great, respected man had leprosy and nothing could be done. He was going to die.

Enter the heroine of the story: a young Israelite girl. She had been grabbed from home and family during one of Naaman's raids on Israel. She had not wanted to leave but she had been captured and brought back to Syria. In fact Naaman was so pleased with her he decided to keep her in his own house as a servant for his wife.

The girl was now living in a foreign land with different customs and culture, against her will. Where was this God who had promised prosperity in Deuteronomy 28? Life was not easy but in spite of all the difficulties she remained loyal and faithful to her God.

Having got close to Naaman's wife she suggested a meeting with Elisha. A meeting was arranged and to cut a long story short Naaman was cured of his leprosy when he took a step of obedience and in faith was washed seven times in the filthy River Jordan for no other reason than that God had asked him to do it!

Naaman would never have been healed in this way but for the faith of an ordinary, insignificant girl who was bold enough to speak out for her God.

Jeremiah (Jeremiah 1)

God had a specific plan for an ordinary young lad from Anathoth in Benjamin who was completely unknown. His

name was Jeremiah. God had actually called this young
person before he was even born to be a prophet to the
nations. The problem was that Jeremiah did not think it
possible that God could use an ordinary young person like
himself. He thought he was too young—and we do not read
that there was anyone around who told him that was
nonsense! His response to God was: "Lord, I do not know
how to speak; I am only a child" (Jeremiah 1:6). In reply
God spoke these words:

> "Do not say, 'I am only a child.' You must go to everyone
> I send you to and say whatever I command you. Do not
> be afraid of them, for I am with you and will rescue you,"
> declares the Lord. Then the Lord reached out his hand
> and touched my mouth and said to me, 'Now, I have put
> my words in your mouth. See, today I appoint you over
> nations and kingdoms to uproot and tear down, to destroy
> and overthrow, to build and to plant."

Do we expect that God could put a similar calling on
someone in our church group?

Mary: Jesus' Mother (Luke 1–2)
It is quite reasonable to expect that the Saviour of the world
would be born into great material prosperity. Yet Jesus was
born in a stable, in poverty. It is quite reasonable to expect
that the Saviour of the world would be born to someone
special. Jesus was born to an unknown village girl, Mary.
  From what we know it is likely that Mary would have been
something like fifteen years old when she conceived of the
Holy Spirit and bore Jesus. Looking round our church youth
groups it is unlikely (and theologically unnecessary!) that
another Mary will be found! The point is that God chose
an ordinary teenage girl to give birth to Jesus. And is it not
possible that he would want to call young people in our
present generation to serve him in a special way today?
  The question to ask ourselves is whether we are doing

enough to encourage those children and young people within our own churches whom God has already called.

The boy with a packet of sandwiches (John 6:1–15)

The feeding of the five thousand is another powerful story with a lot to teach us. I was once asked to speak to a group of lawyers in Plymouth at a lunchtime inter-church meeting. After a lot of thought I settled on this story and taught on faith and expectation within the Church. The lawyers thought they were in for a nice comfortable Sunday school style story, but by the end of the meeting there were some pretty uncomfortable ''vibes'' from some who had felt they could learn nothing new from this familiar passage!

The five loaves and two fish were not much by any standards. When Jesus took them he was able to make something very big from something that had started very small. The secret was that the boy gave all he had. Jesus did not expect him to give what he did not have but he did expect everything that the boy could offer. Had he kept back one of the rolls for himself just in case, no miracle would have taken place. This is such an important principle for adults and children alike. This young lad would certainly have found it easier to take steps of faith as an adult having learned the practical basics as a child.

The most amazing part of the story to me is that the child was absolutely vital in Jesus' provision of the food. Without the child the crowd would not have been fed in that way at that time. When we consider that there were women and children present the likelihood is that perhaps twelve to fifteen thousand people were fed as a result of that boy's faith. What a good job all the children did not have to leave and go to a separate mountain for their own meetings!

Jesus' attitude

Nowhere do we read that Jesus talked down to children and young people. Nowhere do we find any hint of Jesus turning

22

away children on the basis that he had an adult ministry. Jesus was interested in the whole family.

Among his special friends were Mary, Martha and Lazarus, a family group. Jesus took time out to heal Peter's mother-in-law who was lying in bed with a fever. Jairus' daughter was raised to life when Jesus commanded her to get up. In fact with Jairus' daughter Jesus immediately handed her back to her parents once she had been brought back to life, for her parents to give her something to eat. Similarly the man born blind whom we read about in John 9 is likely to have been a young teenager just about at the age when Jewish boys were accepted as men. So when there was some confusion over whether it really was him that had been healed or whether it was someone who looked like him, his parents said, "Ask him; he is old enough, and he can answer for himself" (verse 21).

The well known incident where the disciples tried to rid Jesus from the bother of having to deal with children shows us something specific about the place of children in the Kingdom of God. Jesus said, "Let the little children come to me, and do not hinder them, for the kingdom of heaven belongs to such as these" (Matthew 19:14).

Similarly the equally well known incident of the disciples asking Jesus about who is the greatest in the Kingdom of God brings an interesting response. Jesus actually picks out a child and sets him in front of the disciples and tells them that the greatest in the Kingdom is the person who humbles himself and becomes like a little child. Then he said something very significant. He said: "Whoever welcomes a little child like this in my name welcomes me" (Matthew 18:5).

This must be one of the Bible's greatest affirmations of the value and worth of children. Children are not merely to be tolerated, they are to be welcomed. They are not a peripheral part of the Kingdom of God, they are a central part of it.

Children can teach us so much. They are generally less inhibited than adults and more able to learn without difficulty. Their lives are uncluttered with the cares, concerns, questions and doubts that many of us adults experience. Their faith is simple and straightforward, honest and real. These are very laudable qualities, which we need to learn from. Although it is true that children lack experience, what they have in terms of innocence and enthusiasm still makes their contribution valid.

Jesus explained that the key to being greatest in his Kingdom is to humble oneself to become like a child. Sometimes it is humbling to admit that we do not have all the answers and that we lack experience in many areas. Yet if we are able to do this, and to listen to and take on board what our children are saying and doing, we will actually develop and become more mature ourselves.

Jesus' words indicate that by welcoming children and making them part of what we are doing, we are actually welcoming Jesus and making him a part of what we are doing. All too often I have picked up an attitude in church life which says that children are not really welcome because we want to get on with the grave business of worshipping God in a serious, adult way. This kind of attitude is contrary to the teaching of Jesus.

It is interesting to note that children happened to be around wherever Jesus went. It was easy for Jesus to pull out a child from the crowd for demonstration purposes because children would automatically have been there! That is why Jesus received requests from parents asking him to bless them. It was not a children's afternoon on a busy preaching tour. The children would have been there with their parents as a matter of course. Much of Jesus' teaching with parables and miracles would have been understood by the children and in any event the authority Jesus had would have been appreciated and felt by all ages.

Families

We have already noted that Jesus concerned himself with the whole family and certainly had time for the children. The concept of the family is something which can also be seen throughout the Bible. In fact the family was woven into the fabric of Jewish life. Little systematic teaching would have been necessary because in Jewish culture no one knew anything different.

It is no surprise to find references to the whole family at strategic points in the Old Testament.

One example concerns the children of Israel in the Promised Land. In Joshua 8 we find that the land of Ai had just been taken. Joshua then built an altar to the Lord on Mount Ebal to offer up sacrifices. They stood around the Covenant Box and Joshua read out the whole Law. Verse 35 says, ''There was not a word of all that Moses had commanded that Joshua did not read to the whole assembly of Israel, including the women and children, and the aliens who lived among them.'' Everyone was involved. The whole family was included.

Another example can be seen in the book of Nehemiah. The city of Jerusalem had been rebuilt and when it was finished, Ezra the scribe was brought in to teach the people about God's Law which had been forgotten for many years. Ezra stood up and read the Law to an audience of men, women and the children who were old enough to understand (chapter 8).

In the book of Acts there are many references to people being baptised together with all their household. Once someone in the family had become a Christian, it very often happened that others in the same household would also become Christians and the whole lot would be baptised together. This happened, for example, with Lydia (16:15), the Philippian jailer (16:33) and Crispus the leader of the synagogue (18:8).

In the late twentieth century with a breakdown in the

family unit, the concept of the nuclear family is something which the church is increasingly going to have to reinforce. Statistically we know that more than one in three marriages end in divorce. Many children are growing up knowing nothing of family life and a secure home with two functioning parents. The Church has to come to terms with this reality. That is why it is now more important than ever that we really understand the value and importance of the family unit. We need good systematic teaching on aspects such as family life, fathering the fatherless, building family security and so on.

Within the church family we need a greater recognition of children and young people in the life of the Church. Certainly there is no shortage of biblical evidence to support a higher profile for them.

Chapter 3

Ministry to Children – the Basics

Children have an amazing capacity to learn. By the age of two my little boy Sam had learned all the words as well as all the music to "Rich"—my first album of praise and worship songs. In fact, he seemed to know the whole thing better than me. Certainly, unlike me, he never seemed to forget the words!

Children also have a far greater capacity to understand than we give them credit for. It has been my experience all over the country that when things are explained properly, children can pick up and absorb some very "advanced" teaching. Sadly we tend to play safe all too often and talk down to our children. Is it really any wonder that having been talked down to all their lives they suddenly decide that they do not seem to fit in to church when they get into their teens?

Ministry to children—like ministry to new Christian adults—must of course start at the most basic level. Then, having got the foundations right, we can and should expect to see them going on to greater things. The most basic aspects of Christian teaching should be covered and pressed fully home in order to build a proper foundation.

Becoming a Christian

I became a Christian at the age of seven. I had been brought up in a Christian home and although things later went very wrong in my family I was at that time taught the basics just by watching, listening and having explained to me exactly what the Christian life is all about.

The role of Christian parents cannot be overemphasised. They have an absolutely vital part to play in developing a child's faith. It is the prime responsibility of the parent and not the church to teach children about Jesus. The church should merely support the work that parents are already doing. When Sam was prayed for at our fellowship soon after he was born (we chose to avoid an official "dedication") someone had a prophetic picture of a small tree growing up inside a tube. It was the job of the tube to stabilise and help the tree to develop. It was as though God was saying that our role as parents was to create stability and a learning environment. It is our responsibility to teach our family. It is our responsibility to nurture it and to lead by example. It is part of the job of our fellowship to support what we teach and to reinforce that teaching by offering the benefit of someone else's perspective and approach to the same basic teaching.

I actually became a Christian whilst I was at Crusaders, a Christian youth organisation. I used to love those meetings. At the time they were "state of the art" in terms of children's ministry. Although things have moved on a little since then I still look back and thank God for the influence that the organisation had in helping to shape my understanding of God.

Christian children are special!

In the course of my ministry over the past two or three years I have been the guest speaker at a number of businessmen's dinners. Often the speakers who are invited to these meals have amazing stories to tell.

Imagine the situation. You are sitting in an hotel dining-room, full of good food and coffee, listening to a man who on his flight over from the States (where he has just been) mentioned Jesus to the person sitting next to him. Then before you know it the cabin crew are kneeling in the aisle praying for forgiveness and the Captain is "very interested" in Christian things—and all this before the plane has even taken off! The speaker was previously a drug addict and an alcoholic and part-time arms dealer but now is a Christian and travels the world to speak at businessmen's meals!

Imagine my feelings when asked to speak at my first meeting! When preparing what I would talk about, all I could think of saying was that I became a Christian at the age of seven before I could even spell "sin" and have loved the Lord Jesus ever since. As I thought about this stunning material for my talk I got more and more depressed!

Then an amazing question occurred to me. Who has the greatest testimony: the ex-terrorist who came to the Lord late in life or the ordinary person who since a child has known the love and protection of God for nearly a lifetime? I began to realise that my testimony was not quite as bad as I thought and that in fact I had quite a lot to say!

This whole thought process put everything into perspective for me. It does not matter that I was not a Mafia agent. I have been a son of God from my childhood! I came to realise that whilst others were leading reckless pre-Christian lives I was already safe and sound in God's loving care, sleeping peacefully at night and getting to know a little more about God every day!

What a responsibility we have and what an incredible opportunity we have in working with our children. Both as parents and church we have a clear responsibility to teach children what the Christian life is all about and to teach them how they can come to know Jesus for themselves. We need to teach them how valuable they are to God now, as children, and not as some potential worldwide megastar.

Getting the foundations right

The way we present our teaching about Jesus must be very clear. It is easy to give the wrong impression. We need to be careful about the "love gospel" or else we are faced with difficult questions, like: Who is hell for? We need to be

careful about hell and judgment or else where is the God
of love? The "prosperity gospel" may leave the child or
young person wondering why we still have poverty in the
Kingdom!

Children do need to be taught about right and wrong.
This is not particularly fashionable in the 'nineties when
we are given to believe that there are no absolute standards
and that no one should be able to say that what I am or
do is right or wrong. Yet the Bible is clear that sin has caused
us to become separated from God. We all do wrong things
and children must know that this includes them. An
interesting question at this point is to ask yourself when
you last apologised to your children for something you did
wrong that affected them!

We all choose to do wrong and because God is totally right
we cannot co-exist alongside him in that state. The Good
News is that Jesus has made it possible for us to become
God's friends. He has done all that is necessary to enable
us to choose to become friends with him. He has died on
the cross to pay the price necessary to deal on a once-and-
for-all basis for all the things we do wrong. If we choose
to accept his forgiveness he will come and live with us.

This is the Good News in a nutshell. But there is a lot
more that could be said and which needs to be said. Children
(and adults, too) need also to know the fatherhood of God
and the power of the Holy Spirit. This is the full gospel that
we must teach (and which will be developed in later
chapters).

It is not sufficient to palm our children off with the old
"insurance" theology. This doctrine for years majored on
(to use the jargon) a personal Saviour saving us from our
sins so that we can live for a blissful eternity with him. This
approach sees eternity as the be-all and end-all of
Christianity. It says nothing about relationships, about
enjoying the Christian life, about fellowship together or
maturity in God in this present age—*now*! We must bring

a proper balanced perspective to our children. For many, that means having to come through some of these issues ourselves first!

It is amazing that the Good News of Jesus is so simple that even a small child can understand it. Intellectual ability, whilst a gift from God, has absolutely no bearing on one's ability to become a Christian. Spiritual truth is spiritually discerned not intellectually understood. A child may not understand the difference between a Calvinist and a Universalist but does that matter at this stage? He can know that he is a special friend of God and that all he has ever done wrong is forgiven and forgotten!

When do children become Christians?

The night I became a Christian I remember feeling like I had just had an internal shower. Even as a young boy I felt clean and I knew that something had happened to me. With this in mind I felt quite sad recently when a lady at a church I was visiting said, "Surely you don't believe that children can become *real* Christians, do you?"

When children make a commitment it is important to understand that the exact moment of "conversion" is not always easy to identify. Often children will make several commitments—just in case! As a child of eight I can remember giving my life to Jesus on a number of occasions. I can vividly remember being challenged to the core at an old-style evangelistic meeting held in a tent at Crystal Palace and being convicted of my own sin. On another occasion at around the same time I remember being at a Cheshire Home fête with my parents and grandparents. For no apparent reason I became really challenged about the need to follow Jesus and be a real Christian. All day long and without anyone knowing, I was being challenged and wanted to be sure that if I were to die right then I would go to heaven.

A child's spiritual perception should never be

underestimated. As parents and as church leaders we need to know that God is able to speak into the lives of children and give them a very clear understanding of what the Christian life is all about. Often, in the past especially, we have tended to over-compartmentalise our expectation of outward responses rather than believe that God can be working in a very real way on the inside that may not appear to be too obvious.

At one time I was always keen to know exactly how a person had become a Christian and, more importantly, when! Unless someone could give me a date and a time (or approximate time!) I was sceptical. Now I understand much more that God draws people over a period of time and he sees their hearts and understands where they really are with him. Yet, we tend to go by the outward appearance, and if someone does not use the right evangelical jargon we tend to feel that there is a missing spiritual dimension! Just because someone does not pray "the sinner's prayer" does not necessarily mean that that person cannot have become a Christian.

This was brought home to me in a most graphic way when I led a children's weekend away recently at a conference centre on Dartmoor. There were nineteen children aged between seven and twelve, but nearly half were not Christians. By Saturday lunchtime we had covered the basics and I gave an appeal. No one responded! I was a little disappointed to say the least. One of the organisers was very upset, having had such high expectations of the weekend, and was crying in the kitchen. I went for a walk and prayed for a breakthrough.

That evening I led a session on the Holy Spirit. It turned out to be a very powerful time with most of the children worshipping in tongues and many of them prophesying. I suddenly realised that many of those who at lunchtime had not even responded to a basic appeal for salvation were now away in the Spirit! When all the children had gone to bed and I was drinking coffee with the leaders one of them asked me casually how on earth I sorted all that out theologically!

The answer seemed to me that God sees the heart rather than the outward response. In a moment those children had become Christians and were filled with the Holy Spirit all in one go. The fact that they had not responded to a formal appeal was on this occasion quite irrelevant.

Water baptism

A chapter on becoming a Christian would not be complete without a section on baptism. Baptism is very often a forgotten element, regarded often as an afterthought. Yet baptism is in a sense a part of becoming a Christian. Nowhere does the Bible teach that baptism actually makes a person a Christian. On the other hand we do need to recognise that it is more than a mere outward sign of an inward change. Baptism seals in a commitment that has already been made to Christ. "Repent and be baptised" is the teaching of the Bible (see Acts 2:38). As soon as a person has handed over his or her life to Christ, that person needs to seal in that commitment by being baptised. After all, it is a command!

Just as in the Old Testament circumcision was required as an evidence of what had already taken place in the heart, so under the new covenant baptism is the seal. Romans 4:11, for example, says that Abraham ". . . received the sign of circumcision, a seal of the righteousness that he had by faith while he was still uncircumcised." Baptism is the sign, the seal of our commitment to Christ. It is like signing a deed. At baptism we become signed, sealed and delivered from Satan's kingdom!

It ought to be stressed that I am referring to baptism by total immersion. How can people be baptised to seal in a commitment that they cannot possibly understand because they are babies? Baptism is for the believer, for the person

33

who has already decided to hand his or her life over to Jesus. To sprinkle infants in the hope that it might do something is about as useful as touching a baby with a stethoscope in the hope that it might become a doctor!

It is amazing how upset people can become over baptism. Many people who have become Christians resist baptism. Sometimes it is fear of standing up in front of others to state what has happened in their lives. Occasionally it is a fear of water. More usually it is a fear of other people. Whatever the fear, it leads to resistance. The longer we put off baptism, the harder it seems to get for most people. Clever attempts have therefore been made to give a theological explanation to twist around scripture to create a doctrinal cloak for fear. It all becomes so much more respectable if there is a resistance to baptism which seems to be based objectively on good teaching rather than on subjective fear.

Baptism can be fun! Lynda's baptism was particularly memorable. It was a lovely July day—the sea was grey, the waves were five feet high and it was flasks and blankets on the beach immediately after the meeting before everyone dashed home as quickly as possible to put the fire on! Praise God for swimming pools!

The interesting thing is that God can break through and speak to a person about baptism even in the most unlikely situation. I once led a Saturday evening session for a youth group weekend away at a centre in Devon. In the middle of a short talk I gave at the end of the evening I found myself talking about baptism. I had not planned on doing this—it was not in my notes (or at least wouldn't have been if I had any notes!). I felt a real power in talking about baptism and so pressed the point home. Immediately after the session people began to bombard me saying that God was confirming to them that they needed to be baptised. One of the leaders came over and gave me the usual congratulatory hug and whispered in my ear, "You do realise that this is an Anglican group?" I just wished the floor could have opened up and swallowed me whole! I had completely and quite genuinely forgotten this. In fact I am quite sure that the Lord had deliberately shielded me from the thought because I would never have been rude enough to speak about something provocative in that situation unless I had a clear brief to do so!

There are many people in our youth groups who need to be challenged about baptism. Often we have skated round the subject on the basis that we do not want to push anyone into it (if you pardon the pun). If leaders opt out and say nothing then who is going to explain it all? I was once leading a youth celebration meeting at a large Elim church in Plymouth. Again God began to speak prophetically about baptism to particular individuals. This time it was a church background where baptism was unlikely to have been a sensitive issue. I realised then that what is a very simple step—an act of obedience—is in fact a very difficult step for many new Christians to take. Baptism seems to be a particular hurdle for youth. What a good job that many churches now have properly organised foundation courses where young people and new Christians can learn all about baptism in a local church context.

Children and Baptism

When it comes to looking at children and baptism there are a number of issues to be considered.

It is important to keep firmly in mind what it is that the Bible actually teaches. As we have already noted, baptism is for the believer. "Believe and be baptised" is something we believe and teach. Or do we?

The Ethiopian official in Acts 8 believed as soon a Philip pointed out Christ from the book of Isaiah (which is what the Ethiopian just happened to be reading at the time). As the chariot journeyed they passed by some water and the official said those well-known words: "Look, here is water. Why shouldn't I be baptised?"

Why not, indeed? He was now a Christian. The command of God was to believe and be baptised. It was so simple. Philip did not put his hand in his pocket and pull out a course of twenty-five baptismal classes he just happened to have with him. On the contrary, before you could say "interesting-theological-interpretation" it was all over. He was baptised. He had taken a step of simple obedience to God.

It is an interesting aside to note that there was no one else present as far as we are aware. Often we have insisted that part of the point of baptism is to be a witness to the world. The Bible does not appear to teach this. Any "witness" element is a bonus, but it is incidental to the main point about baptism being a personal response to God to seal in the whole-life commitment made to Christ.

In the context of children it may be helpful to run through the following questions and answers:

1. Q. When does a person become a Christian? A. When he gives his or her life to Jesus.

2. Q. When should a person be baptised? A. As soon as he or she becomes a Christian.

3. Q. Is there any age limit to becoming a Christian? A. No.

4. Q. Is there an age limit for being baptised? A. No. Usually the answer in reality is "Yes" or perhaps "No but . . ."

Often churches have an unofficial period of probation for new Christians in general and children in particular to see whether there is any evidence of a Christian commitment before we baptise them. I was baptised at the age of eleven having been a Christian for four years. Even now it is not at all unusual for a church to insist on a time lapse during which time children are expected to prove themselves. This "wait and see" approach is not strictly speaking biblical.

With no other section of the church do we ask people to prove themselves in this way. If we are satisfied that a true commitment has been made by adults we will normally agree to baptise them straight away.

It was an enormous privilege for me to baptise a boy of eight whose parents were in our housegroup. Leigh had become a Christian at the age of eight and had even gone through the ordeal of convincing the leadership team that his commitment to the Lord Jesus was genuine! On that basis he was baptised. Again it was a cold day and the river was expected to be very cold. With this in mind I went fully equipped with a borrowed wetsuit and put on my kagoul and rainbow flip-flops. I must confess that when I saw the photographs afterwards even I was just slightly embarrassed!

On the same occasion we baptised Libby, aged fourteen, who had just started travelling around the country on a part-time basis as a keyboard player on my team. Libby had come on in leaps (literally!) and bounds (not literally!) She was now prophesying on the stage at our bookings and her spiritual pictures and words of knowledge were really developing. She was surely overdue to be baptised.

Recently I was asked to baptise a boy of nine on a children's weekend away which I was leading. Some of the church leaders were with us on the weekend and the parents (who were in full agreement with their son's baptism) came along as well. Knowing that both the parents and the church leaders were happy about the child being baptised, I was happy to agree. It was great to see this real lad who was perfectly normal—skateboard under one arm, cassette player under the other—wanting to be baptised. It was also very moving to see the other kids not only praying but also prophesying over him as we all hugged in a rugby scrum around him in the nice warm room before we walked down to the river.

The strange thing about that particular baptism was that everyone seemed to be especially keen for me to do the baptising. Feeling somewhat flattered that they were so positive about this I readily agreed. As we were walking to the river I realised that the other leaders still had their socks and shoes on. When we got to the bank they were all happily standing there and I suddenly realised I was going to be involved in a single-handed operation!

I jumped into the water and immediately realised why I had been volunteered! I also realised why the leaders were watching from the safety and warmth of the bank. I gave out a sharp yell. It was freezing! Being something of a wimp I could hardly stand it. My right foot turned blue, both feet went numb and I was dreading someone feeling led to pray or start up a song! It is usually in that kind of situation that someone begins to pray and then gets a little sidetracked and goes on (and on!) to pray for all the missionaries in China. I felt so sorry for the poor lad who although shivering seemed to be faring very well and had proved himself to be more of a real man than me!

Our reservations about baptising children who have become Christians are quite fair. In my experience there are two main areas of difficulty:

1. Dealing with other children
The problem is that if one child is baptised all his friends may want to join in. The original child may have been quite genuine but his friends might be merely jumping on the bandwagon. The argument is that as baptism is an important command of the Lord it should not be undertaken lightly. The child should wait until he or she can appreciate it properly which of course is quite right. How can we deal with this problem?

2. Dealing with the parents
This can also be a little tricky. If leaders say Yes to A because

there is evidence that A knows exactly what he is doing, but says No to B because B seems a little hazy, it could happen that B's parents get just a little upset. If we are in real fellowship with each other the parents ought to be able to accept the leaders' decision on the basis that B's commitment seemed a little unclear. But life is not always as it should be and bad feeling can so easily creep in.

Towards a solution

In answer to these very genuine concerns some churches have made a policy not to baptise anyone under a certain age. The problem is that any age is going to be arbitrary. A fairly mature girl aged nine from a Christian home could well be in a very different league from, say, a less mature boy of eleven from a non-Christian home.

What is the answer? The short answer is that there is no answer. It is clearly a question to be looked at with each individual child. The idea of an age policy is entirely abhorrent to me. If the individual child had made a real commitment and understands what baptism is all about then surely there are no grounds to refuse. If friends then ask to be baptised their requests will have to be looked at on their own merits. If parents get so easily upset with the leaders this could be evidence of rather more fundamental problems which ought to be sorted out anyway.

What if the leaders have reservations?

Sometimes it happens that children want to be baptised, the parents are quite happy about it, but the church leadership is not prepared to do it. This can be a very difficult issue to deal with. If the leaders are not happy with the child's understanding and it is not really clear that the child knows what he or she is doing, then they are right to refuse.

But suppose the child is ready, fully understands the implications, is fully supported by the parents, but is met by church leaders who have cold feet but refuse to get wet feet! This can happen and it leads to frustration and bad feeling. I have had parents come to me with exactly this problem. On one occasion at a national event the parents even wanted me to baptise their daughter while they were all away from their home church. In this kind of situation we need to have our thinking clear. My advice is always the same.

As members of a local church we are in submission to the leadership. (This does not mean heavy discipleship so that you need an Apostle's consent before you can blow your nose!) We are all accountable and need to be responsible. If the leadership refuses to baptise and we disagree, it is much better to abide by their views—even if you think their view in this issue is wrong—than to step completely outside their authority and go it alone. I believe it is more honouring to God to be submissive in spirit and submissive in character than to make a stand and act in an independent way. There is too much independence in the Kingdom as it is!

Don't run away!
Children do need to be taught about baptism. Both parents and church need to make sure that this is covered properly in any teaching programmes that may be run. We should try not to shy away from difficult issues. As leaders we need to make sure that we are not pushing our children and youth into it for our own purposes, so that we can proudly boast that our church baptises Christian children and youth. Rather, we need to provide teaching and a positive church environment so that those who clearly are ready can be baptised without a lot of fuss.

And finally—communicating with children
Communication, whether it is with adults or children, involves two elements: giving out and receiving in. Part of our responsibility as leaders is to give out in a way that will be received in by those we are speaking to. It is a two-way

process and we need to concentrate on both, recognising of course that there is considerable overlap.

1. Giving out

Important factors here will include the language we use, the style of presentation and developing the ability to speak clearly and directly. It is not only a matter of what we say and how we say it, it is also a question of who we are. Our very lifestyles will communicate a lot about who we are and this is actually as important—if not more important—than merely what we say.

There are other factors, too. Body language is something which many of us are completely unaware of but which has a significant impact. Constantly flapping arms, fiddling fingers (with a microphone, Bible, pen, etc.) are all likely to distract. I have often asked my wife to point out any peculiar mannerisms I may have when in action and— surprise, surprise—she does, in considerable detail! Such feedback is very helpful as it enables us to adjust our overall style of presentation to be as appropriate as possible.

The way we present the material is as important as the quality of the material itself. A bright happy approach, seasoned with humour, and which is at all times down-to-earth, will communicate much more effectively than a boring monotone talk which will be punctuated only with children's snores.

The way we present ourselves is also important. Appearance might not be thought of as relevant to communication but actually it says an awful lot about who we are. It is important however that we are ourselves. If we normally wear open-toed sandals and socks and have a neat, regular haircut, it could come as something of a culture shock if next week we turn up with hi-tech boots, hair with highlights, ear ring and denim jacket!

2. *Receiving in*

From the children's point of view, communication will only be effective when they can receive in what they are being given. They need to feel secure in themselves and with their leaders if they are to be affected by what is communicated to them. They need to feel included.

Children are individuals, just like adults. Some will respond to some things while others will react to them. The old saying, ''one man's meat is another man's poison,'' is as true with children as it is with adults. Having said that, it is also true that, generally speaking, children of the 'nineties will respond differently from children of the 'sixties. If our approach is still in the 1960s the children may have trouble receiving it! Often in the past children have been talked down to in a way which is patronising and sometimes embarrassing. We need to communicate with children with respect. Our style and approach should build a good self-image into the children so that they do not see themselves as half-witted pagans who are always being talked down to, but as real people with value and significance. If our approach is straightforward and contemporary, honest yet simple, children are far more likely to receive from us.

Of course children do have different perceptions, levels of understanding and ability to concentrate. All these will affect their ability to receive. Naturally as children get older these things change and if they are to continue to receive from us, our approach must gear up correspondingly. It is not, however, solely a question of age groupings. Other factors such as home background, education, disabilities (emotional, mental or spiritual) will have a profound effect. Also I have found that a properly-structured approach can reach most people, irrespective of age. Whilst this kind of approach is especially suitable for a one-off special meeting, sessions based loosely on age groupings are a must for the regular week-by-week local situation.

In all that has been said about communication there is one vital point that needs to be made. It is not simply a question of approach. This would be to reduce the communication of spiritual truth to a few mechanical principles. Undergirding all of that must be a basic spiritual anointing, so that leaders actually have something to communicate from their hearts, to bring a true experience and understanding of God into children's lives.

Chapter 4

Child Evangelism?

Becoming a Christian is the most important decision anyone can make. Enabling children to take this decision is the most important thing we can do for them. Child evangelism is therefore something we must look at in some detail.

There is a game we used to play as children. We would all close our eyes and then someone would say a word or phrase. The rest of us would have to say the first thing that came into our heads. For example, if the word was "knife" the first thing to come into my head would be "fork". For someone else it might be "operating table". Those with good Bible knowledge and a sense of humour might say "Eglon" (see Judges 3)! It seems to me that so often when we talk about child evangelism we immediately think "holiday club" or "schools work" or perhaps "what did we do last year?"

In our desire to be safe and predictable we love to do something that we have always done and that we feel comfortable with. The trouble is that comfort can be one of our biggest enemies in the Kingdom of God. Sometimes we need to stop and think before rushing headlong into one of our traditional projects. We need to ask ourselves what we are trying to achieve, i.e. what is our goal or objective. Then we need to ask whether we have people with the vision to translate dreams into realities. Next we have to work out how we actually go about it so as to fulfil our objectives.

It is so important to be able to finish what we start. Many of us know what it is like to start things in a fit of enthusiasm and then abandon them only to get fresh enthusiasm about something else which we rush off to start! We need to have the determination to see through what we start. We need to persevere so that we can say, in the immortal words of Magnus Magnusson, "I've started so I'll finish."

Of course it is God who gives us vision and so it all needs to be prayed right through. However, at the risk of sounding terribly unspiritual, I really believe that a lot of concentrated prayer merely for direction should not be necessary. This is because the people with vision have *already* seen from God what is required. It throbs within them. They eat it, sleep it, see it in everything they read in the Bible and hear it at every meeting. God has breathed his living, prophetic word. What worries me is the planning meeting when no one seems to know what to do and when everyone is suggesting different projects so that at the end of the day the only item of agreement is that everyone should go away and pray for vision! If you have not got the vision when you begin to plan, it is highly unlikely that you will suddenly get it just because suddenly one is needed. However, once the vision is agreed then every detail must be prayed through.

As soon as something new or different is put forward in place of something familiar it is often met by these familiar words, "Oh but we've always done it like that . . ." Maybe we have always done it wrong! To perpetuate something that is sub-standard would be even worse than agreeing to do nothing.

Holiday Clubs
I have to be honest and say that, in many cases I believe the holiday club has had its day. It is not that there is anything basically wrong with a holiday club, it is more a matter of association. It is the same sort of argument that applies to the old hymns. There is nothing wrong with them as such (in fact some fantastic words can be found in many of them), it is just that when I close my eyes and think of

singing a hymn it conjures up for me a mental picture of church life as being hats on, heads down, eyes closed and strictly no peeping (except of course when someone is ''sharing'' something, when it is look-up, sit-up and shut-up). It goes with the neat blue carpet, polished pews and embroidered collection bags.

Often the holiday club is extremely old-fashioned in its approach, with the material and its method and style of presentation quite literally dating back to our own parents' or even grandparents' childhood. In an age of microchip computers and fax communication we have to be more up-to-date. Songs like ''Deep and wide'' may have been fine in our own childhood but are rather different from the hip-hop music that many of our children (as well as some of us!) are into.

Having said that, we have to recognise that a lot of good things have happened in holiday clubs. Many children have become Christians at these events, and for many others good seed has been sown. Often the spiritual impact is only appreciated some time later.

The point that is being made is that we need to see God continuing to reach people in an effective way. It is always important to make sure that our approach is relevant and contemporary. Perhaps the time has come for us to reconsider our methods of child evangelism and acknowledge that there are other possibilities in addition to the familiar holiday club concept.

An ongoing outreach

A regular church-based presence in the community will have a far greater long-term effect than a one week hit-and-run evangelism style of a holiday club. *We* know we are still around afterwards but does the public understand this?

So how do we reach children? Having been responsible for leading an outreach project into the community for the two years it ran, I have learned some very important lessons.

At the time we lived in Gunnislake on the Devon–Cornwall border. Our fellowship was based in Tavistock four miles away but as a local housegroup we all had a great vision to reach the community. Nothing was on in the village for children so we began a club at the public hall called the Victory Gang. It was an immediate success. We soon had over fifty coming every week largely from unchurched non-christian backgrounds in a rural village situation. Every week our teaching was overtly Christian but wrapped up in a very fun way. Disco lights, PA system, electric guitars, overhead projector etc. were always a pain to carry around, but it was well worth it. Every child was given a Bible and in time many gave their lives to Jesus.

As time went on I began to travel further afield (in the lead-up to my going full-time) and another couple who were heavily involved moved away from the area. We knew we would have to call it a day. No one else had come forward to take it over and rather than see the whole thing fizzle out to nothing we decided to act positively and bring it all to an end. A letter was sent to all the parents offering transport to enable every child to be involved in the children's ministry at our fellowship. We were anxious to keep the children and see them built into our fellowship instead (unless they were already involved in another church). Not a single child carried on. Not one. Even though we had been there every week—not just a once-a-year holiday event—we lost every single child. I was so disappointed.

Another disappointment was that despite all the talk, all the prayers and lofty ideals, we never formed any real relationships with the parents. Although we were well respected in the community—everyone knew who we were and what we were doing to the point where we had even earned the respect of the local council—we never really reached the non-Christian parents. Some friendships were formed but no more than were formed anyway simply waiting at the school gates. Despite running video evenings, coffee and dessert evenings at a local hotel, and children's presentation evenings for the parents, no real friendships came out of them. Certainly no one came along to the fellowship meetings on a Sunday as a result.

Through all this I believe I learned a lot about children's work and travelling around the country I see the same kind of situation time and time again. Some of the common areas can be summarised as follows:

1. Church base
Probably the most important foundation for children's work is that it must be based in the life of the church as a whole. None of us are called to be lone rangers. We are to be accountable, visible, responsible and submissive. In Gunnislake we were in a rural situation where the fellowship was four miles away in Tavistock. Our initiatives came out of the housegroup. Although we had the encouragement and support of the fellowship as a whole it was not the same. With hindsight we should either have planted a fellowship presence in our village as a proper base or should have operated from Tavistock.

2. Continuity
One positive aspect was that we were always there. Every Monday evening, rain or shine, summer or winter, we would be there. We decided to keep it to term-time only as we found that so many would be away over the holidays, especially the summer holidays. We were able to build up a relationship with the children over a period of time and earned their trust and respect.

A holiday club on the other hand is largely a one-off event. Although the church is still there for the other fifty-one weeks in the year, the people in the outside world do not quickly grasp the link between Uncle Bernie in his clown's outfit on the one hand and the rest of the church (in their

Sunday outfits) on the other! In short, children's ministry is often a hived-off aspect of the church and the children are taught that they are some form of potential for tomorrow rather than an integral part of the church today.

3. Relevance
To be relevant we may have to be radical. Sunday school style flannelgraphs, and "choruses" may now have to give way to a more relevant approach. Humour, contemporary music and fast-moving fun are much more likely to communicate. A move away from video and soundstrips to a "live" presentation where those leading *are* the visual aid is likely to be more effective. Whilst puppets may appeal to the younger age groups the danger is that they are over-used with older ones. A "cool" thirteen-year-old is unlikely to be amused by a Punch and Judy approach.

The teaching needs to be powerful and dynamic as one would expect from a good communicator in an adult context. Children's ministry is often trite and boring. There needs to be a clear expectation that God will work in power and authority.

Children's celebration meetings
With all this in mind it would not be right to say that a one-off event is necessarily wrong. On the contrary, such events will often be the specific high point where a breakthrough is made. The point is that our one-off events need to supplement our regular, ongoing church-based activities.

A children's celebration meeting is certainly a more contemporary method of outreach and is likely to be much more appealing to people outside the culture of the Kingdom! I use this approach regularly and have been very pleased with the results.

For example, I was invited last year to go to Chesterfield to work in various schools for three days. A breakneck tour all over the area was organised for me to do a programme of school assemblies throughout the day. Everywhere we went we advertised the Friday night family Praise Party which was put on at a secular venue with a plush interior, the Winding Wheel. Children were invited to bring parents, friends, relatives, Uncle Tom Cobbley and anyone who could be dragged off the streets! We played to a full house on a very hot summer's evening. Although we had to learn some lessons as a result of this approach it seemed to be a successful way of introducing people to Jesus. A number of people were prayed with to become Christians.

Friendship Evangelism
It would be a bold step for some to scrap traditional child evangelism *per se*, but maybe we need to think it through for a moment before allowing inbuilt prejudices to react and say No! We are hearing a lot nowadays about friendship evangelism. The idea is that the church should be moving away from the big evangelistic event once a year and working instead with friends and workmates on a low-key but fifty-two weeks a year basis.

Of course one of our biggest difficulties in friendship evangelism is that many of us in the church do not have very many non-Christian friends to evangelise!

The idea is that adults would bring along their friends from work or the people in their street. If they eventually give their lives to Jesus and join the church their children will be there too. Children also could bring friends from school and from the neighbourhood to the main programme meetings of the church—either on a Sunday morning or during the week at the various children's meetings. This would result in automatic and ongoing contact, based in the church.

Obviously we would like the meetings to be good! I know what it is like to suffer the embarrassment of taking a non-Christian to a meeting and then be sitting there regretting it! However I have discovered that even in that situation God can still be at work.

50

We once took the non-Christian husband of a Christian friend to a housegroup in circumstances where if it went wrong we might never see him at at the fellowship again. We felt it was a make or break situation. It turned out to be the worst housegroup I have ever been to. I can say that because I was leading it! Nothing seemed to gel and the atmosphere was heavy and miserable. Praise and worship were feeble and everyone was tense because we had a non-Christian with us. The very next day he became a Christian, to everyone's amazement and excitement! It is reassuring to know that God is much bigger than our perception of how the meeting went.

Reaching the whole family

If we concentrate on winning adults for Jesus they will bring their children with them because they will join the church as a family. It is true that when they arrive at the doors of the church we immediately break the family up by throwing the children out of the meeting and down a dingy corridor to Sunday school. But at least they come as a family.

If we concentrate on children the reverse is not true. It does not normally happen that they bring their parents. Some will but most will not. With this in mind there is a strong argument for saying that we should perhaps be thinking more in terms of reaching the whole family together rather than splitting it up and trying to reach members of the family individually.

There are times when a particular emphasis on child evangelism may well be right in the context of a particular church situation. There is one church in Kentish Town, London, where I have led meetings on a number of occasions that has a special child vision. The whole church, its leaders and workers have a vision for reaching inner city children where family life is the exception rather than the rule. The church is doing a fantastic job. Their work involves a sacrificial lifestyle and I have been personally challenged in looking at the cost of their commitment. Whilst it would be wrong to copy a successful initiative without specific vision, that church has a lot to teach us about ongoing child evangelism.

Restructuring the Church
The suggestion has already been made that a church can be restructured to concentrate more on the whole family. This will be developed more fully in Chapter 15. Suffice it to say at this stage that a true family emphasis in the church will lead to adults, children, youth and singles all feeling that they belong.

Wider issues
In thinking about evangelism—whether it is with children, adults or the whole family—it is important to consider not only the type or style of our approach but also some of the wider issues about people.

1. *Understanding individuals*
We need to be able to understand what is happening in spiritual terms to people on the inside. We have tended in the past to concentrate our evangelism on the meetings rather than on the people. A better understanding of people as individuals and the reasons why some respond whilst others react, may help us to see evangelism as a commitment to leading individuals to Jesus rather than a commitment to putting on meetings!!

2. *Spiritual warfare*
Some people may be held by spiritual bondages. We know that our fight is not against flesh and blood but against principalities and powers (see Ephesians 6:12). The most effective weapon to combat this is prayer and spiritual warfare.

Our prayers for individuals we meet who are clearly in

bondage can bring them to the point where they begin to reach out and ask for help. Very often when we pray it seems as though nothing is happening but I have found from experience that it is in these times that God is at work on the inside. We should not get fed up and give up, we must persist in our prayers. Interestingly enough, spiritual bondage can be found in children just as much as with adults.

At one recent event where we were working with teenagers we found that beneath the ordinariness of the external appearance lurked real spiritual bondage. But, having said that, appearances can be deceptive. Just because someone is uninterested, apathetic and opting out does not mean that he or she is being oppressed by evil spirits. On the other hand I have found it to be not uncommon for a fairly ordinary activity such as worship to stir up all sorts of spiritual forces that were not particularly apparent in people's lives. At this particular event most of the ministry centred on healing and deliverance. It was great to see teenagers being set free from demonic power when prayed for. The manifestations were not very pleasant but the sense of peace and authority when individuals were delivered was very positive indeed.

3. *Adaptability*

In all that we do that makes up ''evangelism'' we are called to be adaptable. That is why in just one chapter, Acts 28, we find Paul using a variety of different ways of reaching out to people on the island of Malta. First he meets up with some primitive people. Soft words and fine intellectual argument would have been about as appropriate as a pork pie at a Jewish wedding. His approach was to use signs and wonders. When they saw that Paul was unharmed by a poisonous snake which he shook off into the fire, they changed their minds from thinking he was a murderer and thoroughly nasty chap and said that he was a god!

In the next verse Paul comes across Publius, the leading citizen of the island, who had a large estate. He was wealthy, intelligent and good at entertaining guests properly. However, his father was desperately ill and this was his point of real need. So Paul prayed for the man and he was healed.

A little later in Rome Paul called the Jewish religious leaders together. On this occasion his approach was to explain and persuade from the Old Testament scriptures from morning to evening (see verses 17 and 23).

The interesting thing is that we do not read that revival broke out! Paul may in fact have been seed sowing, but at least he was completely adaptable to real people in terms of their own culture and spiritual perception.

When our evangelistic initiatives are not relevant it can be terribly embarrassing. I once spoke in a hotel at an evangelistic dinner for businessmen. The meal was good, the coffee was good, I hope the talk was good, but the embarrassment was the praise and worship. The problem was there was only one musician and he was not very competent. The songs were old and the style reflected a traditional church sub-culture that was about twenty years behind the times. Asking non-Christian businessmen to sing is bad enough, but asking them to sing sub-standard Christian songs without an atmosphere of powerful anointing made me wish there could have been a convenient trapdoor in the hotel floor from which I could have made an unobtrusive escape! One wonders whether praise and worship were appropriate at all in this context.

The principle of adaptability holds good when we are dealing with children and the whole family just as much as with our adult initiatives. Are draughty village halls with paraffin heaters, tubular steel chairs with most of the canvas backs fallen apart and dirty wooden floors really suitable venues to show the generosity and love of God in action? Add to this the traditional approaches of Auntie Bertha's glove puppets and Mr Thistlethwaite's slightly-out-of-tune nylon-strung guitar and one has a perfect recipe for disaster!

In our approach to evangelism it is essential to keep in mind that children as well as adults are individuals. They have different attitudes, backgrounds and perspectives. All of us are the product of situations and people that have affected us and shaped the way we act and think. We are a blend of both the people and events of the past on the one hand and our own characters and personalities on the other.

Individuality cannot be ignored when it comes to planning evangelistic programmes. We need to take into account in particular that the children will be at different stages in their level of understanding and perception of Christianity. Our approach must reflect this.

4. *Commitment and aftercare*
Evangelistic talks tend to concentrate on that thin band of time when a person makes a commitment to Christ. The reality is that people will probably have to hear a clear presentation of the Good News several times before they will be in a position to respond. And, as noted above, it may be necessary for spiritual bondages to be broken.

Once a person has made a commitment it is, of course, only the start, not the end of the story. There must follow effective discipleship training and a release of gifts and ministries. Often, especially with child evangelism little thought is given to this. We are generally more concerned with "hit-and-run" evangelism and chalking up decisions than in building up disciples. To achieve a lasting result we need a strategy for dealing with individuals after the event. A lack of after-care will render all our public success of limited real value. We will have built nothing of lasting value if individuals are allowed to slip through our fingers.

Pulling it all together
From my experience as a local children's leader and more

recently from my experience nationally, I believe that if we are to be successful in child evangelism we need a much more contemporary approach. We need to portray a fresh style and ethos in the Kingdom and show the church to be a caring and relevant body of people. Above all, or course, we need to show Jesus.

I also believe that the time has come to review our vision and to ask whether our time, energies and attention could perhaps be better used in reaching out to the whole family rather than to individual children.

Changes to the structure of church life will be inevitable if we are going to take seriously the call to reach out to others with the Good News of Jesus. Jesus humbled himself and became a man so as to identify with and reach out to real people in a way which was relevant. Too often we expect people to adapt to our traditions and preferences. Maybe the time has come for us to be more like Jesus—to humble ourselves and be more culturally relevant so that we identify with and reach out to people in a real way.

Chapter 5

Providing the Right Church Environment

When children make a commitment to Christ it is vital that we as church provide the right spiritual environment in which the child can grow and develop. In fact it is important that we provide the right environment before they become Christians as well, otherwise they could get a warped view of what it is all about and decide they do not like what they see! They may not even hang round long enough to know what it is all about!

Role of parents

While talking about children in the church there is an important point that needs to be made straight away. This will be a crucial backdrop to everything that we go on to say about the church. We need to understand that the primary responsibility for teaching children rests not with the church but with parents. The church has a vital role, but it is one which supports and undergirds what is taught at home.

The reason for this is clear. Children spend their whole lives around the home. They go out from home to school, to play, to church, to cubs or brownies, to the shops. They always come back home again. Home is the focal point of their whole lives. Being a Christian is a whole-life commitment. There is a Jesus perspective to school, a Jesus perspective on videos, a Jesus perspective on outings, homework, holidays and everything else that goes to make up life. Christianity as a lifestyle (and *not* a religion) needs to be rooted in to the reality of everyday life. There is only one category of person that can possibly do this: parents.

As a Christian parent I have to face up to the fact that if my son chooses not to follow the Lord in his own life, whatever the reasons and background I cannot blame my church and say in effect: ''It is your fault.'' As parents we are the ones to shape lives, offer encouragement and bring in the Jesus view on everyday issues.

It follows from this that we have a tremendous responsibility to shepherd, guide, encourage and provide for our children. This book is not about children in the family, it is about children in the church. But we need to bear in mind that the children in our churches have a home context. It is the parents' responsibility to take their role seriously. It is the church's role to build on that in a corporate context.

We need also to bear in mind the situation where a child comes from a totally non-Christian home and turns up at the church without Mum or Dad. Perhaps in this special case we as a church must accept more responsibility as we are his or her only reference point for real-life Christianity.

The style of the Church
In providing the right church environment for children to develop we must look behind the veneer of church life to the reality of what is underneath.

I am convinced that what causes separation and division between various churches is not doctrine. We all believe the basics. Although we may emphasise certain aspects we all believe the same basic doctrinal package. Yet looking round at our various streams and denominations or non-denominations, our churches are actually very different. Why is this?

I used to think the difference was simply over the issue of the Holy Spirit. I thought that once individuals had been filled with the Spirit and the leadership was moving in a generally Spirit-filled direction, all would be well. After all it is the Spirit himself who leads us into all truth.

Since I have been in full-time ministry travelling all over the country, and now with an increasing amount of overseas travel, I realise that this is simply not the case. I have to be honest and say that I had always assumed a non-denominational "House Church" would almost by definition be good. Then I went to a few! I now know that even here, there can be struggle, hassle, heaviness, oppression, frustration and bondage. Thankfully it is not all gloom and doom—far from it—but I have had to learn a lesson. Just because there is an emphasis on renewal and restoration does not of itself provide an instant recipe for success!

So what is it that causes our vast differences if it is not doctrine? I believe it is all a matter of style and ethos. In the words of the old song: "It's not what you do it's the way that you do it." So also in the church. Also "It's not what you believe it's the way you believe it" which will make a difference. It is that certain something, that indefinable element that can only really be summed up as style and ethos which causes us all to be different. We may have two churches described on paper. Both can have a similar leadership structure—but they will have different leaders. Both may teach freedom of paise and worship— but different perceptions of what that means in practice. Both may teach about the Holy Spirit—but with very different levels of personal experience. All of this will be reflected in the style of church we grow.

I was recently invited to lead some sessions for children and the whole family at a large well known Baptist church. The Saturday evening session went extremely well. Many children and young people were filled with the Holy Spirit and were worshipping in tongues and prophesying. Some adults were reaching out in these areas for the first time as well which was great. The problem was Sunday. I was asked to do nothing "charismatic" and nothing which could be vaguely interpreted as likely to upset some of the "older" folk! Yet the minister himself told me that he is Spirit-filled and worships in tongues—on his own in private, that is! This was to me a perfect illustration. No doubt the gifts of the Spirit (to use one example) are preached from the pulpit. The minister is Spirit-filled, yet the style and ethos of the church is very traditional indeed.

When we examine our children's work against this background we see that what is caught is as important as what is taught. In some churches the only thing children are likely to catch is a cold! Yet that church can have a very similar doctrinal position to another where things are happening. Children's needs will best be served in a church environment where not only is the teaching good (this should go without saying) but where the style and ethos is right. A good church should be like a car with power steering—light and positive! This is so important when we remember that we are talking about training a whole new generation that needs to feel a part of what we are doing in the here and now.

The style of our churches will have an important effect on the success of our ministry to children and young people. However, it is a fact that our most radical mark 10 supersonic fellowships have been no more successful than anyone else in keeping young people when they get to their teens.

This indicates that it is not solely a matter of style and ethos. There is a real need to examine the structure of our churches as well.

There are a number of issues which relate to style and ethos which directly affect our children's perception of "church". These will be looked at individually. Whilst it is true to say that the style is set principally by church leaders, it is hoped that the following comments will be of help also to those with a responsibility for children's ministry.

1. Passivity

We are living in an age of passivity. Apathy is "cool". Enthusiasm is out, being passive is in. It may possibly have something to do with factors such as the video age (not that there is anything wrong at all with video!) which makes no demands of the person to be entertained other than to put the tape into the slot and switch on. We can have everything we want without hardly ever having to lift a muscle.

I recently led a series of meetings in Worcester, one of which was for youth. Everyone wanted to lounge round on the floor! No one was really that fussed about praise and worship. It was okay provided they could choose to opt out! I gave a short talk during which I knew that God was speaking to individuals. But when an opportunity was given for ministry and praying for people not a single person responded! As soon as the meeting was over, there was a steady stream of individuals who wanted me to talk and pray with them on issues relating to alcoholism, sex, rejection and so on.

I am finding this kind of response—or non-response—to be fairly typical. At one time young people had the reputation of being radical, noisy and lively. Now they are bored, switched off and miserable with hardly a spark of life to share between them.

But passivity is not confined to youth. I am often involved in leading whole family celebration/praise party events which are open to all ages. I always encourage adults to join in and go for it, yet so often they try to slip to the back to opt out. I make a point of making chairs available to the elderly and those with doctors' certificates only! People go to unbelievable lengths to sit down passively and opt out!

If our youth and adults are so often difficult to motivate, what chance do the children have in breaking into real freedom? The only leadership examples they see around them teach them to switch off and opt out! The strange thing is that adults seem to expect children to be naturally bouncy and happy, enjoying a good bop to praise songs as if it were a natural phase that they are expected to grow out of with maturity! Is it really any wonder that many of our children in the church are bored, apathetic, pedestrian and totally switched off?

Wherever I travel I find that the elements of joy and enthusiasm are so often missing from church life. In fact these qualities are somewhat frowned on and thought to be unspiritual. They are perceived to indicate ''froth and bubble'', a lack in substance and shallowness. Enthusiasm is tolerated among the little kiddies in the church but not with adults. But if under the Old Testament covenant David managed to dance and whirl before the Lord when the Ark of the Covenant was brought back to Jerusalem (2 Samuel 6), how much more have we got to be joyful about under the new covenant! The problem is that the church is not full of Davids, it is full of Michals—people who see others dancing before the Lord with all their might and despise them in their hearts (see verse 16).

Of course we all talk about having the joy of our salvation, but when asked where it is we are likely to say that it is that deep joy which is deep down in the heart. In fact it seems to be so far down it probably would no longer be able to remember its way out into the light of day any more! The feeling is that demonstrated joy is superficial and irreverent! I have been met by the following well-worn response so often that if I had just £1 for every time I have heard it I would now be into prosperity with a capital P! People often say that they have had to endure real hardship, hurt and difficulty in their Christian lives. Real hardship, they say, means you cannot make a shallow response but you can retain joy and victory in your heart! The point here is that we have all been hurt from time to time. We all endure difficulties. We all know hardship. It is what you do with it that makes the difference. The person who says, ''I will press through and praise God right in the middle of my troubles,'' is the person who truly understands victory and is being mature in it. If things are getting tougher, we should be getting sharper!

Sometimes people look at me and think that I am an extrovert, an exhibitionist, always pulling someone's leg, having a good laugh. They conclude that I never have any problems. The fact that I may have been misunderstood, slandered, dumped, financially exploited and so on do not appear to count as real issues. The truth is that we are all in this thing called the Christian life together! We need to develop more resilience to problems so that we are not all the time allowing every little thing to get us down. We need to allow the joy and enthusiasm God has given us a chance to jump out!

If we, as God's people, will not reflect that side of God's personality which shows joy and enthusiasm, who will? Jesus said (Luke 19:40) that if his people would not praise him he would call the very stones to cry out in praise to God. The church will soon need people with a ministry of wheeling wheelbarrows—to bring all the stones into the meetings! This is not to say that we should always be in perpetual joy with false plastic smiles. But it does mean that our church life should be undergirded with a basic joy and enthusiasm.

Children need to be shown, by example, that passivity is not honouring to God. As adults we have a responsibility to lead children into genuine joy and enthusiasm which will give them a different perspective both on the church and on life in general. Whilst we must never be afraid of teaching them about silence, this really is not the issue. Many of them know all about that already. Now is the time to bring happiness, joy and enthusiasm into church life.

2. Heaviness
It sometimes seems that in the Kingdom of God we love heaviness! We feel safe with it. We feel secure with it.

Certainly we feel very familiar with it. The only problem is that it is giving our children a totally wrong concept of what the Kingdom is really all about.

It is as though we have confused spirituality and heaviness. We have come to believe that if we want to become really spiritual we must become really miserable! The more holy we are, the more miserable we must be.

As a child I was brought up in a church I perceived to be like that. By the time I was nine I had counted every plank of wood on the walls and had counted every ceiling tile. Several times. As we all sat in a holy silence waiting for the next person to say something I would amuse myself by listening to the clock ticking. It was about as exciting as watching paint dry. I was bored. It was quiet. It was predictable. It was miserable. It was heavy. I remember thinking that there must be something more to church than this. After the meeting people would speak in hushed tones until clear of the front door. Once outside everyone became normal again, laughing and joking, speaking in their real voices rather than in evangelicalese, talking about everyday things.

The question to my young mind was this: Why do ordinary, real, Christian people actually make it all so heavy for themselves inside the meetings? It is a question I have never really been able to answer!

More recently as I have travelled around I have found many churches and fellowships that have had some experience of renewal, yet choose to stay in heaviness. A good barometer of this is, of course, the children's perception!

Picture a meeting with an aura of quietness. Some put their hands over their eyes as though praying. Others bow their heads and look pensively at the floor. In the quiet someone cuts in with what used to be called a chorus (usually an old one!) just to do something. There is an unexpressed feeling that this is all being terribly holy, that somehow we are creating a suitable atmosphere for the Spirit to move. The reality, of course, is that it is heavy and miserable. Often the children will have left for Sunday school by this stage in the meeting so that we can get on with the "real business" of worshipping God. The children are a distraction and a hindrance to worship which the adults cannot wait to be rid of.

By contrast, imagine a fellowship situation that is completely different in style and ethos. Imagine people being natural, talking without jargon (as far as this is possible!) and being friendly. An atmosphere which is light, yet charged with anticipation and excitement. A place where children are positively welcome and where they can have input. A place where the worship is genuine, properly led and powerful. Imagine a meeting where everyone is involved, where the Spirit is doing his work yet where people are joyful, thankful and enthusiastic. Imagine an atmosphere of real fellowship more akin to being at home in the kitchen than at a hat parade.

Is all this too idealistic? The answer is no. It is quite achievable if the leadership has a vision for it and is prepared to work hard over a period of time to achieve it. It will involve cost, heartache, an inevitable loss of individuals on the way, but it is certainly possible. That is not to say that every meeting will be brilliant, but the general style and ethos will change for the better. In a sense we owe it to our children to create an environment which will encourage them to prosper in their own lives and ministries.

A heavy, religious image does very little for anyone, least of all our children. sometimes it is the little things that say the most about where we are. At a church I went to in the north of England at a special children's celebration event with lots of children milling around before the meeting, I was horrified to see a notice outside the minister's office which read "Quiet please. Prayer meeting in progress." What kind of message does this give to our children? It tells them that their presence is being tolerated not welcomed, that the real business is going on in the office and not in their meeting, and that to succeed spiritually we must have total silence, not a lot of running around. No wonder so many children feel excluded, unwanted and outside the church family.

It is possible to give a wrong impression to our children unwittingly. At one event when the leaders were praying before the meeting (a little practice that is universally thought to guarantee spiritual success) the children were being repeatedly told to go away because we were praying!

3. Unworthiness
In the Kingdom of God I have observed what can only be described as an unworthiness mentality. It is an attitude that says we are so unworthy; we cannot do anything; we have no valid contribution to make; no ministry; no hope; no friends—only gloom and depression!

It could be argued that unworthiness is just another name for lack of confidence, and that church is a safe place to say we feel it. Certainly we all lack confidence in certain areas, especially when we are stepping out into new areas. But the unworthiness mentality goes further than this—it suggests that we are no good and will never be any good.

What is worse, the concept soon rubs off onto our children so that very soon they too think they are no good. The truth of course is quite the reverse!

I first noticed this as a child. Week after week someone would get up in the meeting to pray. The prayer would go something like this: "O Lord, thou knowest I have nothing to commend myself to thee. If only I livest as I know I oughtest to live then all would be well. But I know I have failed thee, let thee down again and again, even this week, and am wretched in thy sight. Now please help me to live better and not to fail thee . . ." It was actually years later—once I could understand the jargon—that I really understood the heart behind the prayer. The interesting thing was that I had noticed my own prayers were taking on a similar form (without the thees and thous). I felt a failure, always letting God down, unworthy, not living to the standard I thought I should be. All in all I began to realise I was living in total condemnation and utter defeat although of course I would not admit it. Many of us are like this, often without even recognising it. Children are catching it, too. How can we escape and, in particular, how can we rescue our children?

I found I had to go back to basics and find out what the Bible said God thought of me. I began to realise something significant. The Bible told me that I was separated from God because of my sin and that there was nothing I could do to re-establish links with him. It also told me that all my righteousnesses were as filthy rags and that there was no good thing in my flesh. But then I met Jesus. All of those previous things are now in the past. Now, as a son of God, I realised that I am free from all that! God has made me totally accepted as I am because I now belong to Jesus. So while it is quite true to say that before I was a Christian I was totally unworthy *it is not the case any more*. I realised that I must stop believing the devil's lies that said I was still unworthy.

I am convinced that many Christians do not fully grasp the concept and scope of grace. We all know that it was Jesus who took the initiative and that it is nothing to do with our works that we are Christians. Yet when we look around in the Christian world it seems that although we are saved by grace many subconsciously think that we then carry on by works. We tend to think that what we do will earn God's favour. So, for example, most people will think they do not read their Bible enough, do not pray enough, do not tell others about Jesus enough, do not give enough, and so on. Then as a result we begin to feel guilty and then condemned. Sometimes we make promises to God about praying more or reading the Bible more. When we fail we have broken promises to add to the already long list of failures!

To avoid being misunderstood I need to make it clear that reading our Bibles, prayer and so on are essential for spiritual growth. I would be the last person to suggest we give these things up. But when the realities of daily life mean that we occasionally miss a chapter we should not feel that tomorrow we owe it to God to read two chapters to catch up!

Consider the effect of all this on our children. So often these feelings of unworthiness are handed on and the next generation grows up feeling condemned almost before it starts. One issue that needs careful thought in this context is the danger of over-teaching the basics to children. Let me explain what I mean.

Usually we concentrate on the basics when it comes to teaching the children. If Samuel (who ministered to the Lord as a priest even as a child) were in our churches he would be shunted into a side room and asked to make a model of Noah's ark using the inside of an old toilet roll and a yoghurt pot! We often do not work at releasing the potential gifts and ministries in children, preferring rather to stay with the familiarity of the basic gospel message. The problem is that having laid the foundation we need to build on it. If we continually teach salvation to children who have already made a commitment they will grow up thinking they know it all, and have heard it all before. And because they keep on hearing that they are sinners and unworthy of God's love, they also grow up with a slightly distorted view of the truth and see themselves as having very little self-worth or value. The unworthiness syndrome is therefore reinforced.

4. The Sunday mentality

It is amazing how different we can be on a Sunday! Suddenly it is as though someone has thrown a switch and we go into religious mode. I often notice the difference when I lead a meeting on Saturday evening and then again on Sunday morning.

At one fellowship I visited recently we met on Saturday evening in a village hall for an all-age family celebration. It was one of those all-singing-all-dancing sessions (literally) that I love. It was a packed hall (a little unusual for me!) and everyone was going for it. The children were bopping away, and so were the adults. One child got so excited she sprung a leak. The atmosphere was terrific and the presence of the Lord was powerful. As it happened on that particular occasion more ministry went on with the adults than with the children. Adults were stepping all over each other to bring prophetic words. Words of knowledge were flying around, one guy was prayed for to be healed of a stomach disorder. It was all happening! The evening was a great personal encouragement and everyone seemed pleased.

Twelve hours later we were back in the same hall with the same equipment. Most people at the meeting had been at the session the previous evening and I was ready for action. It went down like a lead balloon! The worship was lumpy, there was no response to the preaching, the atmosphere was heavy. The contrast was stark. I knew exactly what was causing it—Sunday mentality. Jeans were off, skirts were on. Suddenly this was "church" and had to be accompanied by a holy heaviness.

Although this was in one of the new churches (which used to be called House Churches) the same attitude can be observed in all churches. I have seen it time and time again.

What does this teach children? It says to them in effect that we regard Sunday as a special day, a holy day that is set apart and which demands us to act in a completely different way from normal. Whilst I would never wish to upset anyone who, before the Lord, keeps Sunday special (and whilst incidentally I believe that one day off a week is essential) I do feel that we need to ask ourselves whether the Sunday mentality is being helpful either to our children or to us. If we are not careful we begin to give the impression that Sunday and Church are separate from the real world—

that the Christian bit of my life is somehow separate from the rest of me. We then end up seeing a divide between the secular and the spiritual rather than seeing ourselves as one indivisible person.

Our children need to know that there is not a Christian pigeonhole and a rest-of-me compartment. They need to know that they are just as acceptable to God whilst they are outside playing on their bikes as they are at church meetings singing action songs. God is with them every bit as much when they are at school as when they are praying with Dad before bed.

5. *Kingdom organisation*

Another important factor in creating the right spiritual environment for our children is what I refer to as Kingdom organisation. It would be more appropriate sometimes to call it Kingdom disorganisation! Our children can easily run away with the idea that the Kingdom means sloppiness.

I always aim to start my sessions on time (or the customary five minutes late which is expected at concerts) but usually I am asked to wait for a few moments extra as the bus from Blanktown has not arrived yet. On one occasion in the south-west of England a busload arrived literally half-way through the session—and everyone thought this was normal! Sloppiness so easily creeps into our fellowships. If the meeting is supposed to start at 10.30 there is no one there. So we wait ten more minutes. The people who were late think they might as well stroll in late next week as they did not miss anything. And before we know where we are the rot has set in!

It is not only with timekeeping that we can be sloppy. I remember leading a regional youth celebration meeting in Plymouth. I had not taken a band but was using local musicians. A rather spectacular keyboard arrived, which seemed very promising. It got to half an hour before blast-off but no one had arrived to play. By now I was becoming a little anxious. The start time arrived. No keyboard player. I started anyway. The keyboard player never did turn up. It looked a little strange to see everything set up but no one to play! A similar thing happened once in Southampton when the drummer turned up ten minutes before the start time.

I have led several seminars where someone thought about taping the sessions only at the last moment. My experiences here have ranged from someone literally running down the road to Woolworths to buy some batteries, to someone popping back home to get a simpler cassette recorder they could operate without a degree in electronics!

Being efficient and well-organised is not a substitute for spirituality, but it is important. There is an enormous variation in the standard of efficiency, organisation and image among Christian organisations. The sad thing is that an organisation that may be doing great things can have its reputation completely tarnished by poor administration.

The church should not be characterised by sloppy attitudes. It is important that our children take church seriously in the sense that they understand they are actually dealing with God's own Kingdom and get their thinking into gear accordingly.

Chapter 6

Children and the Holy Spirit

All too often the church views its children as unevangelised pagans. Week by week basic teaching is given about what it means to be a Christian. It is rare to find churches which have caught a vision to see far more achieved in the lives of their children.

By and large the church does an excellent job in building basic foundations. Most churches which are going anywhere at all will work hard to ensure that their children know the basics of salvation. And it is vital that children are taught this. If they do not grasp the basics, anything they try to build will be about as successful as the foolish man's attempt to build a house on the sand.

The problem is that few churches take the children on from there. Having built a good foundation we spend our time going over the same ground all over again. All we are doing is building another foundation on top of the solid foundation we have already built.

Children's workers appear to believe that children can only understand anything if there is something to look at. No one seems able to bring any teaching without an object lesson. Adults scratch their heads each week trying desperately to think up (usually late on Saturday evening after anything good on TV!) some amazingly clever visual aid that will impress everyone. As time goes on it seems that we are getting more and more competitive, with everyone trying hard to out-do last week's seemingly unbeatable performance. Each Sunday we have wheeled into churches all aver the nation items such as glasses of water, dog food, electric food mixers, computers, golf clubs, umbrellas, the inside of an old toilet roll—you name it, someone has probably used it!

The question is: does it all communicate? Of course it entertains—and there is nothing wrong with that—but does this approach really communicate at the level of need in the lives of the children?

I can remember on one occasion listening to an adult preacher who was excellent. What he said really spoke to me. It was powerful and made an impact. He preached from John 3 and although it was a word for adults he put up a huge umbrella at the front of the church to illustrate what he was saying. Looking back now I can remember the umbrella but I have absolutely no recollection as to what the point was or even what he was preaching about.

In my experience many children have had enough of the basics and now want more in the way of solid food. Children have an amazing spiritual perception and a fantastic ability to learn and to apply what is learned. Many of our children hunger for more. They have a genuine faith and they are crying out to be stretched and to have their faith shaped and developed. The tragedy is that we refuse to meet them at their point of need and prefer to stay with the basics. We choose to stay with what we know we can handle behind the smokescreen that after all they are only children.

As a result there are many children in our churches who are growing up feeling they know it all. They rapidly realise that even as children they have heard it all before, seen it all before, understood it all before. They are over-familiar with the basics. They are bored. They become "switched off" until in the end nothing seems to touch their lives. The fact is that the Kingdom of God is furnished with children who spend the meetings counting the number tiles on the ceiling, looking out of the window, wondering how much further the big hand on their watches will have to travel past home time before they will actually be on their way home. Is it any wonder that when children reach their teens they are off? Perhaps the wonder is that they are not gone sooner!

The time has come to see our children equipped. I would like to buy every church leader a tee-shirt which says on it: "Children are people too". So often our churches do not treat them as people. We do not see them as possessing gifts, ministries and abilities already. We are not working hard to encourage their gifts or creating a safe environment for them to begin to exercise their gifts. Instead we perceive the children as a nuisance. Underneath the pleasant exterior and after we have said all the right words, the reality is that we can hardly wait to get shot of the kids into their own meeting so that we as adults can begin the real business of worshipping God, on our own, in the "main" meeting. May God hold a mirror up to our eyes so that we can see what we have done and so that we can see our children the way God sees them.

What is the answer to this? How can we give our children value and significance? More to the point, how can we convince the church that its children are actually part of God's strategy for revival rather than some peripheral nuisance?

Part of the answer lies in the way we minister to children, but part of the answer also lies in seeing effective leaders emerging and in changing the structure of the church to accommodate renewal amongst the whole family. These issues are so important that separate chapters will be devoted to them.

For now, bearing in mind that most of us have to take the church as it is (and not as we would like it to be), we need to see our children equipped properly. We need to see them filled with the Holy Spirit and beginning to use the gifts of the Spirit. This will be the first step in actually building something on the basic foundation we have already laid.

Baptism in the Holy Spirit—an introduction

Many books have been written on the Holy Spirit. Many cassette tapes are available on the subject. A great emphasis has been placed on the work of the Holy Spirit. Yet in spite of all these teaching resources there are many, many people who are still struggling with the basics and who long to be released in the gifts of the Holy Spirit for themselves. We have become a people with a lot of knowledge about the gifts but not very much practical experience. If we are not as yet there ourselves, we will never be able to teach our children.

I want to be as practical as possible in dealing with this very important topic. The theology and doctrinal basis will be covered only in outline. There are many good books on the subject already. The major emphasis will be on how we can see it all happen in practice. Many of the realities which one only discovers the hard way and which are never preached about will be covered specifically. The aim is to blow away the mystical super-spiritual ethos surrounding the baptism in the Spirit and to be down-to-earth and as practical as possible.

Is the Holy Spirit optional?

We have to understand that the Holy Spirit is not an "it" but a "he". He is part of the Godhead. He is God. He is not merely a spiritual influence. Therefore when the Bible encourages us to be filled with the Holy Spirit it is asking us to be filled with God himself.

The Holy Spirit is not a bolt-on extra for keen people, a kind of spiritual accessory for the enthusiast. Sometimes in the past we have perceived the Holy Spirit to be for the people who decide to opt for the Ghia specification of Christianity rather than the ordinary "L" pack model that most of us are happy to put up with! However, if we could get along quite happily without him why did God give him in the first place? If we leave him out of the equation we become unbalanced. We become like a car firing on only three cylinders. The sad fact is that we have got so used to the sound of a misfiring engine that we have come to think of it as normal!

Children need to know that the Holy Spirit is for them and that he wants to give us all the power to enable us to lead effective Christian lives. In this generation our children need all the equipping they can get!

The Holy Spirit in the Old Testament

Because the Holy Spirit is part of the Godhead he has always been in existence. The first indirect reference to him is in Genesis 1 when (verse 26) God said, "Let us make man in our image, according to our likeness . . ." The Hebrew word for God, Elohim, is a plural word. The Holy Spirit was there at creation.

Throughout the Old Testament period the Holy Spirit is referred to. Under the Old Covenant he would come upon someone for a particular purpose to get a specific job done. It was almost as though he made a special guest appearance at important times. There are many examples of this, the following being a random sample.

Othniel: "The spirit of the Lord came upon him so that he became Israel's judge and went to war. The Lord gave Cushan-Rishathaim king of Aram into the hands of Othniel who overpowered him" (Judges 3:10).

Jephthar: "Then the Spirit of the Lord came upon Jephthar. He crossed Gilead and Manasseh, passed through Mizpah of Gilead, and from there he advanced against the Ammonites" (Judges 11:29) before making the rash vow to the Lord which cost him his daughter's life.

Samson: "The Spirit of the Lord came upon him in power. The ropes on his arms became like charred flax, and the bindings dropped from his hands" (Judges 15:14).

Saul: "When Saul heard their words [the threat of Nahash the Ammonite], the Spirit of God came upon him in power, and he burned with anger. He took a pair of oxen, cut them into pieces, and sent the pieces by messengers throughout Israel, proclaiming, 'This is what will be done to the oxen of anyone who does not follow Saul and Samuel.' Then the terror of the Lord fell on the people and they turned out as one man" (1 Samuel 11:6–7).

"[Saul] prophesied in Samuel's presence. He lay that way [naked] all that day and night. This is why people say, 'Is Saul also among the prophets?' " (1 Samuel 19:23).

The Old Testament itself taught that there was coming a day when the Holy Spirit would not be given on an *ad hoc* basis to a selected few, but would be poured out in a general sense. The prophecy of Joel looked forward to a time when God would pour his Spirit on all people (see Joel 2:28–32).

When we come to the New Testament the stage is already set for an altogether different approach. Jesus had already promised his followers that the Comforter (the Holy Spirit) would be given once Jesus himself had ascended to heaven. Immediately before his ascension Jesus reminded his disciples about this and told them to wait in Jerusalem for the promise to be fulfilled (Acts 1:4). It was while the disciples were waiting in Jerusalem, meeting in the upper room, that the Spirit was poured out.

The promise of the Holy Spirit

After the Holy Spirit had been poured out in Acts 2 and the disciples spoke in tongues and prophesied, many people were swept into the Kingdom of God in a huge blaze of evangelism. As people were becoming Christians Peter said something very interesting. Having explained about repentance and baptism, he said: ". . . And you shall receive the gift of the Holy Spirit. The promise is for you and your children and for all who are far off—for all whom the Lord our God will call'' (Acts 2:38–39).

The promise of the Holy Spirit is therefore to all Christians including children, i.e. as many as God calls. This promise therefore reaches down to us at the end of the twentieth century.

If we believe that all Christians have the promise of the Holy Spirit, the promise becomes claimable as soon as a person becomes a Christian. We can therefore expect to see a person becoming a Christian and being filled with the Holy Spirit both at the same time. I like to think of it all coming together as one package deal.

If it should happen that a person becomes a Christian as a child rather than as an adult, it makes no difference as far as the promise of God is concerned. Children are still people and if children genuinely give their lives to Jesus they become Christians. If they become Christians the promise of God is to them. It is as simple as that!

As soon as I saw this in the context of children's ministry I began to get very excited. Suddenly I had received a scriptural authority for something which was already beginning to stir deep within me: children can and should be filled with the Holy Spirit! I realised that I needed to teach this and to expect to see it happen. I could hardly wait to put it all into practice!

When Jesus taught his disciples about the Holy Spirit he said this:

''If anyone is thirsty let him come to me and drink. Whoever believes in me, as the Scripture has said, streams of living water will flow from within him. By this he meant the Spirit, whom those who believed in him were later to receive. Up to that time the Spirit had not been given, since Jesus had not yet been glorified'' (John 7:37–39).

The only pre-condition of receiving is to be thirsty. If we want to be filled we can be, however young (or old) we are, because God has promised!

Am I filled with the Holy Spirit as soon as I become a Christian?

This is a difficult question. The answer appears to be both Yes and No! It is the Holy Spirit who first shows us that we do wrong and that we are separated from God because of this. It is the Holy Spirit who draws us and who leads us to Jesus. When we ask God into our lives the Holy Spirit comes too because he is God.

Having said this, we need to recognise that in New Testament times at least many of the early Christians had not been filled with (or baptised in) the Holy Spirit. When the Christians met together in Acts 1 and 2 they already knew the Lord Jesus. They had met together for prayer and fellowship. They were all with one accord, one purpose, in the upper room. The problem was that until this point the Holy Spirit had not actually been given, or released, in a general way. On the Jewish feast of Pentecost the time was right from God's point of view and the Holy Spirit was poured out generally.

After this when Paul arrived in Ephesus he found some Christians there and asked them whether they had received the Holy Spirit when they became Christians. They replied, "We have not even heard that there is a Holy Spirit" (Acts 19:2). Paul explained everything, prayed for them and they spoke with tongues and prophesied on the spot.

The only instance recorded in the New Testament where any of the disciples were asked to wait to be filled was Acts 1 which we have already looked at. This is simply because at that stage the Holy Spirit had not been poured out in a general way. That did not happen until chapter 2! At that stage God was not ready. From chapter 2 onwards God has been ready and has never asked anyone to wait again! The only reason why the disciples in Ephesus had not received the Holy Spirit was simply a lack of teaching. As soon as Paul supplied the teaching and prayed for them, they received the Holy Spirit straight away.

There is a big theological debate as to whether we receive the Spirit as soon as we become Christians or whether being filled is a subsequent experience. The problem is that whilst the arguments rage many ordinary people are no nearer to being filled with God's power. We need to make sure that in addressing the issue we do not get so wrapped up with the theology of it that we completely by-pass the personal experience of it!

If we think it through logically there is no reason why a new Christian should not be filled with the Holy Spirit immediately. The best plan is to see them becoming Christians and being filled with the Spirit all in one go. I have experienced this with children as well as adults.

While leading some seminars for church leaders recently in Zagreb, Yugoslavia, I was told that as soon as people become Christians there, they are encouraged to speak in tongues immediately, and they do. If the words of Colossians 2:10 are true, that we are complete in Christ, then as soon as we come to Christ we are already complete and quite capable of launching out into the gifts of the Spirit provided we are taught how to. The problem is that by and large new Christians do not receive this teaching and they then become like the disciples in Ephesus who had not even heard of the Holy Spirit. For them it has to be a subsequent experience because no one taught them that they were already filled when they gave their lives to Jesus.

When we explain all about the Holy Spirit to children we do not need to go into these theological niceties. They are not interested and it may confuse them. All they need to know is that the Bible teaches it, God has promised it and we need to experience it. Then as soon as they are led into it they will immediately start to use the gifts in a simple, uncomplicated way simply because no one has ever told them it is controversial and hard!

An introduction to the gifts of the Spirit

When we are filled with the Holy Spirit, God has a number of free gifts to give us. This is a very special offer! 1 Corinthians 12:7–11 tells us that there are nine gifts:

* Word of Wisdom
* Word of Knowledge
* Faith
* Gifts of Healing
* Miracles
* Prophecy
* Discernment of Spirits
* Tongues
* Interpretation of Tongues

Anyone looking at some charismatic churches might be forgiven for thinking there are only two gifts: tongues and prophecy. Yet God wants us all to be fully equipped and reaching out for the other gifts, not smug and self-satisfied with the basics.

It is important to understand the nature of the gifts by first-hand experience so that we can pass it on to the children on the basis of our own experience. In the next chapter we shall be looking at this in detail. For now it is important that we have a general understanding of the gifts.

1. Gifts not wages

The first important point is that the gifts of the Spirit are gifts and not wages. When we work, our employer is in our debt. He owes us the wages we have agreed to work for. With a gift we are owed nothing, it is and entirely voluntary, free-will present.

People sometimes think that the gifts of the Spirit are only for the mega-spiritual! We may feel that we are not holy enough to qualify for the gifts. We then fall into the trap of thinking that we must therefore wait until we are more mature, more holy. What this attitude is saying in effect is this: If I can prove my spirituality to God he will reward me with the gifts of the Spirit. In other words, I can earn my right to them.

All this is, of course, nonsense! As soon as we become Christians God sees Jesus in us. At that moment we become totally accepted in his sight. We are suddenly completely acceptable not because of what we have done to earn it but by God's grace. He took the initiative and the moment we accept Christ, he sees us as holy. There is nothing we can do—God has already done it all—the bill has been paid in full. We cannot earn God's acceptance because we are already fully accepted! If we are God's children and fully accepted we begin to understand that all the gifts have in fact already been given to us on a plate. All we have to do is believe it and start exercising them!

The disciples were ordinary, unlearned men. When the power of the Holy Spirit was poured out it was a risky business. It was like putting dynamite into the hands of children. Part of the problem we face is that we tend to like everything to be cut and dried, neat and in its place. If we launch out into the adventure of life in the Spirit we could have our neatness disturbed. But, as has been rightly observed, it is always messy in the nursery and always nice and neat in the graveyard!

It is vital that children understand this. They need to know that God is waiting with free gifts that are there for the taking! Children need to know that it is not a question of being holy enough, or being old enough, because the gifts are just that: gifts. It always amazes me how quickly children pick up the feeling of unworthiness and condemnation that adults often feel. At a very early stage they pick up that they are not good enough, not holy enough, always let God down, and so on. When it comes to exercising the gifts they need to have a thorough understanding of just what a gift is.

2. Tools not toys

Another vital principle is that the gifts are not charismatic toys to be played with, but tools for us to work with. When I was younger I wanted to use the gifts so that I could show everyone how spiritual I was! I did not understand that using the gifts was not a mirror of my own spirituality. I thought everyone would be terribly impressed if they could hear me worshipping in tongues. I also have to confess that I quite liked the idea of being able to prophesy. I would imagine myself in a big meeting surrounded by people suddenly receiving a most significant word from God so that everyone would be amazed not only at the word itself but also the fact that it was me who brought it!

Now of course I am older and wiser. Yet if I am completely honest there is still a residue of that attitude that I need to keep bringing into subjection!

When I first started nervously to step out in the gifts, God showed me in a little picture something that I have never forgotten. I saw my toolbox (finished in blue enamel and rust) open with all my tools in it. As I looked I saw a large brand new screwdriver gleaming at me. I knew at once what God was trying to say to me. He was showing me that although I had some tools there were more that he wanted me to use and gain experience with.

As I thought it all through I began to realise something significant. The gifts of the Holy Spirit are like tools in a toolbox. When we are filled with the Spirit it is as if we are presented with a toolbox full of different tools. They are all there waiting to be used. Even though we may not be too familiar with some of them it is only a matter of practice until we can grasp the basic skills and become fully competent.

I began to see that each tool has a different job. It is no good trying to use a spanner when a screwdriver is needed. Similarly it is no good trying to use a screwdriver when a hammer is needed. The truth slowly began to dawn on me.

I should not be asking God which gifts he wanted to give me—he wants me to have the lot! In fact I need all the gifts to be able to cope with every situation. If I did not need them it would not be necessary for God to give them to me to equip me. I knew from bitter experience what it was like as a student trying to keep my old Mini on the road with little more than a hammer, spanner and screwdriver in my toolbox. There were times when I needed a specialist tool and had to take the car to a garage simply because I did not have the right tool to enable me to do the work.

I have found that children easily understand the difference between tools and toys. They understand that the gifts are to help us to do work and not to play with. Once they have this perspective they understand the context in which their gifts are to operate. Hopefully they will be balanced and sensitive in exercising the gifts knowing that the object is not merely to show them off.

3. Sticking at it
Sometimes people appear to raise an eyebrow when I say that we need to practise the gifts to become competent. I have never heard this taught, but it is true. It needs to be taught. As we continue with tongues, for example, it becomes easier and our vocabulary becomes wider. As we persevere with prophecy we gain confidence and are able to launch out more easily without all the agonising preamble with God as to whether it is me or God or whether now is the right time to bring it, or whether my sweating palms have got anything to do with it and so on!

If we consider that the gifts are like tools, we know that we can never pick up a totally new tool and use it like an expert. It takes time. It all takes practice. There will be a few mistakes. If we give up on the tool as soon as we make a mistake we will never get anywhere. Mistakes are not to be feared. They are there to be overcome gradually as we gain more experience.

Sometimes we can look at a new tool and realise we have never seen anything like it. When I first saw a tappet adjuster I did not even know which way round to hold it! When we think of some of the gifts like deliverance or discernment of spirits we sometimes wonder whether we will ever be able to master them. If we are patient and prepared to step out when God gives us the opportunity, we will become more experienced and competent.

Children especially need to be taught it how it is. They need to know that their new tongue (for example) needs to be practised so that it becomes a part of them. But we must be careful not to give the impression that if we do not practise we will lose the gift and God will take it away! It is simply a matter of encouraging children to get used to their gifts.

There is one very important reason why practising the gifts is important. It is simply that the more proficient we become, the less we have to think about the mechanics of the gift and the more we can concentrate on the message behind it.

Imagine the following situation. You are in a meeting and feel that you may have a prophecy. You are not too sure whether it is genuinely from God or whether it is from you. It feels a little vague. You definitely feel that God wants to say something but you are not quite sure whether what you had in mind is just for you or whether it is for the church. It could in any event be wrong and it could be that God actually wants to speak to the church through someone else! While you are wiping the sweat from your hands you notice your heart is beating fast but you are still not sure whether what is in your mind is from God. You hope that one of those people who normally give those long detailed prophecies will come to your rescue and say something that will confirm that yours was right after all. While all this is going on, a leader suddenly jumps up, closes in prayer and a coffee is thrust into your hand just as you are beginning to come to the conclusion that the prophecy was right, after all!

Proficiency in the gift will lessen the risk of everyone missing out simply because we are not sure whether the gift is from God. It will enable us to tune in to hear God, pick up what he wants to communicate and speak it out in faith. To put it another way proficiency will enable us to concentrate on God without having to concentrate on the gift.

In the specific context of children, practising is important. But they cannot practise unless there is opportunity in the church for children's gifts to be exercised, encouraged and developed.

4. *Being specific*

Once children begin to use the gifts of the spirit the next step is to see them develop to become more specific. A bold declaration in a large meeting that "there is somebody here with backache" is quite likely to be true according to the law of averages, without a word from God! As we begin to focus more specifically on what God wants to say, and as we have our faith developed so that we are prepared to speak it out, so we shall be able to pinpoint and focus on particular areas more effectively.

Recently I have been teaching on becoming specific in the gifts of the Spirit. It was encouraging to see, at one conference this year, someone on stage state, "There is someone here, in the central section of the meeting, aged 13 who comes from London" with a particular need! I was so excited! Here were children receiving direct and specific words from God. Later when someone said that there was a person present with trouble with their mouth, I asked him to pray for a more specific word. Back came the reply, "It's a girl, she's 13, she's in the blue team and it's trouble with teeth." Sure enough one person responded—exactly fitting that description!

At another event a young teenager came forward to say that there was someone in the meeting with cancer. The tent we were meeting in suddenly went completely quiet. No one responded and a little later we finished the meeting. The next day I found many of my team praying for a lady who had asked for prayer—for cancer. I later learned that the lady had a daughter in our meeting. She had come to collect her on the previous evening and at the exact moment she walked into the tent heard the word of knowledge. Her cancer had been diagnosed only three months previously.

With all the gifts of the Spirit it is important first of all simply to make a start. Once children begin to get a little experience it is then important that the words they bring become specific enough to speak to the particular situation. There is nothing dramatic in being specific in itself, but in being specific needs will be identified in a way that can then be met, or a word can be given that will speak directly into a person's situation. Most of us are not quite so familiar with the idea of children worshipping in tongues or bringing prophecies as we are with adults. We tend to know only traditional ways of "ministering" to children. The time has come for us to move on from perceiving children's ministry as the making of a model of the Temple using old cardboard boxes. We must give time and space to encourage the use of the gifts.

Naturally this means that the children's leaders themselves need to be proficient in the gifts. Any leaders struggling here should perhaps turn straight over to the next chapter quickly before someone notices!

Chapter 7

Children and the Gifts of the Spirit

A question which is frequently asked is this: "Do I have to speak in tongues (or exercise any of the other gifts) to know that I have been filled with the Holy Spirit?" This question is sadness itself. It reveals an attitude which is really asking: "What is the bare minimum I need to be involved in to convince myself and show others that I am Spirit-filled?"

This is like looking down a telescope from the wrong end. The issue is not whether I must struggle into tongues or prophecy (for example) to prove myself. Rather, the issue is what new gifts can I now exercise *because* I have been filled with the Holy Spirit. A minimalist philosophy pervades the Kingdom in so many areas, which is concerned with how little I can get away with rather than how much I can be involved in!

In practice I have found this to be an adult problem. With children all one needs to do is to light the blue touch paper and retire. The kids will go off like a rocket on their own! If you teach them what a prophecy is and then expect them to receive one, they will! If you teach them about tongues and then expect them to speak out, they will! If I then qualify this by saying that it does not always work out, immediately we adults become more interested in those cases and retreat into the familiarity of failure rather than push at the frontiers of success.

The Holy Spirit is available to Christians who are prepared to reach out and accept him. The free gifts come automatically. I believe it is quite possible to be filled with the Spirit without exercising any of the gifts. To put it another way, it is not necessary to speak in tongues to prove that we have been filled with the Holy Spirit. However, what on earth is the point of being filled with the Spirit if we do not use the gifts? It is like filling a car with petrol and asking whether we have to drive it away just to prove that it has petrol in it.

In this chapter we shall be examining four of the gifts in detail. The aim is to be as practical as possible so that children will be able not only to understand it all but to respond and use the gifts for themselves.

Seeing children filled with the Holy Spirit

It is worth stressing right from the start that there is no such thing as a special formula for success when it comes to seeing people filled with the Holy Spirit. What follows is a format for praying with children which I have developed over a period of time as I have travelled around the country. I do not always do it in the same way and it must be borne in mind that in the context of an inter-church Celebration the approach is of necessity "from the front" rather than in, say, small groups.

Whatever the method, I have discovered that it is vital for the leader to have genuine faith and expectation that something will happen. If the children see that you are uncertain and not confident that anything will happen, it is quite likely that nothing will. However, the leader must always be honest and genuine. If you have no faith but pretend you have, the children will see straight through your carefully constructed smokescreen.

When praying for children to be filled with the Holy Spirit I would normally expect them to speak out in tongues straight away. This is because it is important to get started with the gifts and if a good start can be made with tongues, we can move on to the other gifts without too much difficulty.

89

The first thing to do is to give some basic teaching on the Holy Spirit being God's power to enable us to live powerful lives. I would normally teach the promise of Acts 2:39 and explain that the promise is to them and that they can be filled with the power of the Holy Spirit now—they do not have to wait until they are adults.

It is important to have some sort of appeal so that a child is reaching out personally to be filled with the Spirit. Not all children want to be filled with the Holy Spirit immediately. We must never push anyone into something they are not ready for. Some children may not understand fully, others may find it all too new to know quite how to respond. Some children may already be Spirit-filled. The important thing is to give the opportunity but not to push. I never prolong an appeal. It gets embarrassing and heavy and people start to feel awkward and children especially get bored.

In the context of a meeting I always ask the children who have responded to reach out to the Lord right where they are. I never bring them to the front in case they run away with the idea that it is me that is giving the Holy Spirit rather than God! Having said that, it is of course necessary sometimes to pray for some children individually. Laying on of hands when someone is prayed for to receive the Holy Spirit is biblical and right but I would normally do this only when necessary on an individual basis after the meeting.

I have found it helpful to ask the children to close their eyes and literally reach out with their hands to Jesus. Normally I would pray from the front and ask the children to invite the Holy Spirit into their lives while we are all praying together. I would then explain that having asked for the Holy Spirit they will receive, and that in fact they need to believe they have received even if they feel no different.

Before getting into tongues I make a point of explaining that one of the jobs of the Holy Spirit is to release worship in their lives. Having prayed we would then sing a worship song and expect to see the Holy Spirit breaking down barriers and releasing the children in worship. It is amazing the difference this makes. The pressure to get into the gifts is off and everyone can relax into worship and allow the Holy Spirit to begin to do his work in us.

At a well known national conference a team of stewards kept turning up in our venue. When I asked them why they kept on coming to children's meetings their reply quite shocked me. They said that they felt more worship and power in the children's meetings than they did in the ''main'' sessions! I am sure that the adult sessions were actually very good but I was interested to learn that even outsiders could sense that God was doing something special with the children in releasing them in worship. To me the raised hands and the smiles on their faces say it all. We should never underestimate the potential that there is in children's meetings.

This is often a good time to see children released in dancing and movement to show their worship in a positive way. Contrary to many people's natural assumptions, children do not necessarily leap around spontaneously, enjoying their praise and worship without a care in the world. Sometimes they can be rigid, cold and unresponsive. Much depends on the church environment they are used to and the encouragement (or lack of it) from parents and leaders. Sometimes it is necessary to see barriers broken down. Although we will have been working at this through the whole meeting we have to be ready for them to change now that they have received the Holy Spirit.

Tongues

We have an enormous responsibility in seeing children released in tongues. The way we go about it is crucial. We can be responsible either for seeing it all happen or for putting children back years!

As a young teenager desperately trying to get into the gifts myself, I was put back years. I went into the "Side Room" after church with lots of others to "wait" for the Spirit of God to mysteriously "drop" on to us. There was a single line of plastic, stackable chairs set out and I decided I would sit right on the end hoping that the pastor would start with me. In the event he started at the other end!

As he prayed for each person in turn I was very interested in what I saw happening. Some people spoke out in tongues immediately. They were well away praising God in their new praise language. Others were clearly struggling a bit. They had one or two words but nothing like the fluent torrent of words the others had. With others still, nothing seemed to be happening at all. I was wondering exactly what would happen to me!

I decided to look very spiritual and bow my head and close my eyes. Suddenly I felt two large hands descend on my head and so I fastened my seat belt and got ready for take-off! There was one slight snag. Nothing happened. After a while I was asked to stand up while the pastor prayed again. Nothing happened. I was asked to sit down and was prayed for again. Still nothing happened! Now in desperation, I was asked to take a deep breath. Then another. Still nothing happened. During that session I was standing up, sitting down, breathing in, breathing out, doing everything except standing on my head and still nothing happened. I was so disappointed.

Then whilst the pastor was demanding that I spoke in tongues I did something terribly unspiritual. I opened my eyes to peep. I could hardly believe what I saw. There right in front of my mouth, poised like a heavenly microphone, was the pastor's ear! What made it worse, it was a hairy ear. Suddenly the difficulties I was having in speaking out in tongues seemed to get a hundred times worse as I was being asked to perform. I closed up completely, sat down and was very close to tears.

Over the next few months, which then stretched into years, I was prayed for so many times I felt I was in danger of going bald! It was actually five years later at the age of eighteen while I was driving my Mum's Mini late one night and was listening to a tape on the Holy Spirit that I decided to try yet again. I switched off the tape, began to worship the Lord and made a deal with him. I agreed that whatever came into my mind I would speak out as part of my worship. If it was tongues, that would be great. If it was just me—so what? I would still worship God with it anyway.

I spoke out the few strange sounds that came into my mind but what happened next took me by surprise. Even though it was dark and there was no one else around I felt really embarrassed. I thought I was making it all up! It was not exactly fluent. I kept repeating the few basic sounds I had and I thought that somehow I must be missing out on some super-dynamic spiritual experience somewhere along the line. What I had just experienced seemed too down-to-earth and too ordinary to be tongues.

A little later I asked one of the leaders in my fellowship to pray for me. In his back room—where Grandpa usually lived—I received a few more words and a lot of encouragement. Also this man whom I held in such high esteem suddenly became "John" rather than "Mr Smale" and I knew that I was on my way!

Looking back now I thank God for this experience. Had I slipped immediately into tongues right from the start, I would never have been able to identify with the many, many people I have met since who were having trouble with the gifts. My response would have been to give them pat Christian answers in a cold, almost academic way. Now, however, I feel I can be of positive help. I have prayed for many hundreds, perhaps thousands, of people of all ages and seen them filled with the Holy Spirit and starting to use the gifts. Without that experience I believe my own ministry would have been far less effective.

Nowadays I never put people under pressure to perform. When leading a Celebration meeting I normally ask people to sing in tongues first while we are singing a worship song. We all sing it through a couple of times and then I ask everyone to carry on singing but this time in their new tongue. Those who already worship in tongues get straight on with it and the others who have just been prayed for will normally join in straight away as well. This is because no one is watching them! Everyone is concentrating on Jesus and worshipping him and everyone is launching out in tongues anyway. No one feels vulnerable, threatened or exposed.

The first time I tried this out with children I saw it as something of an experiment! I felt strongly that it was all very biblical. I knew God *could* do it. I wanted to believe God *would* do it. I had seen other people do it but what about me? Would it actually work in practice in my own emerging ministry?

It was a regional Celebration Bank Holiday weekend at Lincoln. Ishmael was leading the teens and I was responsible for the nines to thirteens in a separate tent down the road. After the first night's basic teaching where a few became Christians I was ready for action! I did some very basic teaching on the Holy Spirit (from the life of Saul, as it happens) to provide a proper and biblical context to the ministry. Clear teaching is important. To my surprise there was a huge response to the appeal so I prayed for everyone where they were. All over the tent the children began worshipping away in tongues. It was all so powerful, yet so natural and genuine. When I asked them to put up their hands if they had spoken out in tongues for the first time, I was amazed at the number of hands going up all over the tent. The interesting thing was that they were still ordinary red-blooded kids because as soon as we had finished the ministry, they started pinching and kicking each other as normal!

What happened that night sealed it for me. I knew that my work among children and young people would never be the same again. Now I expect to see God at work in the power of the Holy Spirit wherever there is an open heart and a conducive church environment (which, of course, is another story!).

Sometimes people say that all this is all right for me in the context of a Celebration, but what about the usual local church context with, say, a handful of kids? How can we make it happen there?

The answer is that it really can happen there, too! I was once asked to lead a youth meeting at an Anglican church. We arrived early and set up in what, frankly, appeared to be a disappointing size hall. I have since got used to these! When everything was ready and we started the programme the customary five minutes late, I became despondent. Looking out at the crowd I counted a total of fifteen people! I wondered whether we should chop out the programme and do something else but decided to press on. At the end we had a huge response to the appeal—in percentage terms, that is. Seven or eight were filled with the Holy Spirit and were speaking out in tongues and some of these were prophesying as well. The meeting could easily have taken place in a lounge, with similar results. Ironically it filtered back to me that some of the people in the church were furious that young people were now beginning to use the gifts because most of the adults had trouble even understanding what they were all about.

I always try to be very sensitive to the local church situation. I never exceed my brief when I am asked not to cover something. I will never try to sneak in B when I have been asked to do A. Furthermore, I always check out with the local leaders what I am going to do because I would expect them to support me. However, it does not always work according to plan! One slightly embarrassing incident occurred once when praying generally for a group of children to be "filled with God's power" (carefully avoiding the mention of tongues). One girl immediately burst out in tongues and we had to explain what had happened as the words were not on the overhead projector screen!

When praying for individuals, whether children or adults, I try to give them some friendly advice if they seem to be having trouble with tongues. I tell them not to keep trying, but to go home and then when they are alone to begin to worship Jesus and speak out as an act of faith those funny little sounds that will come to mind. Normally this will do the trick.

Whenever I explain the gift of tongues I find it helpful to mention the following points. They help people understand and respond positively. I wish someone had explained it like this to me as a young Christian. As it is I have had to learn the hard way and I am therefore keen to help as many people as possible so that they can learn from my own mistakes and misconceptions.

1. *It is your voice*

I used to think the Holy Spirit would somehow come upon me and speak through me in a very special, holy way. No one ever told me that as it is my voice I have to decide whether to speak out or not! Just as in English I have to decide to speak, so with tongues. It is *my* vocal chords, *my* apparatus.

Similarly I used to believe that if God wanted to give me the gift of tongues he would. I was expecting some unique "special delivery" from heaven if, but only if, it happened to be God's special will for me. No one told me it *was* his will. I was expecting God to do it all. Suddenly I realised that the Holy spirit is a gentleman, he will not barge in and give me something I did not want. I had to want to speak out. I had to be active in seeking after tongues. The truth is that many of us are spiritually passive. We shrug our shoulders and say that we will put up with it if God really wants us to have it but we are not prepared to seek actively ourselves! Yet Luke 11:10–13 says this:

> "*Ask* and it will be given to you; *seek* and you will find; knock and the door will be opened to you. For everyone who asks receives; he who seeks finds; and to him who knocks, the door will be opened. Which of you fathers, if your son asks for a fish, will give him a snake instead? Or if he asks for an egg will give him a scorpion? If you then, though you are evil, know how to give good gifts to your children, how much more will your Father in heaven give the Holy Spirit to those *who ask him.*"

In actively seeking rather than passively waiting we must be prepared to step out with our own voice. We must simply tell our children that it is up to them to decide to go for it and that it will be their own voice!

2. *Am I making it all up?*

Everyone I have ever asked has said that when they first spoke in tongues they thought they were making it up. The problem is that hardly anyone admits to this. If you say it in a meeting you can almost hear the sighs of relief as people realise that they are quite normal and that it happens to all of us!

We try sub-consciously to project a really spiritual self-image. To admit that I thought I was making it all up could mean that someone else now thinks I am less spiritual than they used to think! The fact is that thinking it is our own made-up tongue is a natural part of the process. I always like to forewarn children about this. Then when they feel they are making it up they will know that we all feel like that and so they will not worry that there is something seriously wrong with them.

3. *Stepping out in faith*

Tongues involve stepping out in faith and going for it. Once when I tried windsurfing my brother-in-law explained the principles of it to me in shallow water. I knew the time was coming when I had to launch out in deep water and go for it. It is a strange sensation to lean back into the wind—it is against one's natural instincts. The only reluctance on my part was the fear of doing something wrong which could land me in trouble!

It is the same with tongues. Apart from the unfamiliarity we all experience at the beginning, many of us are gripped with fear. We fear doing something wrong. We imagine all sorts of horrendous consequences which could land us in trouble. And we do not want others to look at us and realise that we have made a mistake. We may prefer to stay with the familiarity of what we know we can handle and avoid things like tongues which could be too risky.

Speaking in tongues always requires an element of faith. We have to decide to launch out and go for it. That is why it is so important to create the right environment to encourage people to step out. With children this is why singing a worship song to the Lord and then going over into tongues can be much easier for them than praying individually, waiting for a performance and being disappointed when they are too rigid with fear to step out!

Doctrinal aspect of tongues

Some people find an important distinction between tongues for private prayer and worship on the one hand, and tongues for public proclamation on the other. I must say that I have never been keen on this distinction and feel that it may be misguided.

The tongue I use around the house, in the car, at a meeting or wherever I am worshipping privately, is the same one as I use when I stand up in a meeting and give a tongue in public. It is not that God gives us a different tongue for a different occasion, rather it is a different occasion God gives for the same tongue!

There are times when it is right to express your own heart publicly. Sometimes it is not clear why. However we must bear in mind that "public" tongues will be interpreted so that everyone in the Church will know what I have said— including me.

This will be examined briefly under the section on interpretation of tongues. It is mentioned at this stage because I do not believe it is either necessary or desirable to explain all this to children at the point of their initial experience. It makes the whole thing complex and cumbersome and may give the wrong impression that speaking in tongues is hard, surrounded with doctrinal difficulties and suitable only for adults. Children will have quite enough to take in all in one go; let us not make it unnecessarily cluttered.

Prophecy

As soon as tongues have been covered it is important to move on to the other gifts. The temptation is to stay with tongues, basking in our success, and not to go through it all over again with the other gifts. The good news is that once the gift of tongues has been properly mastered it becomes easier to move on to the others. It is a natural progression to cover prophecy next.

There is a lot of confusion and woolly thinking over just what prophecy really is. I have found that there are many adults who, if they are really honest, are not too sure what it is. If we do not understand it, how can we pass it on effectively to children? I am going to suggest a rough, working definition.

Definition

Prophecy can be understood as follows: "Prophecy is me speaking out what I believe God wants to say."

In the Old Testament prophecy was not limited to this but also involved foretelling the future. As a gift of the Holy Spirit prophecy, although possibly having to do with the future on some occasions, is much more concerned with *forth*telling what God wants to communicate rather than *fore*telling the future.

Here again experience has taught me some important characteristics about prophecy, summarised as follows:

1. *General feelings*
It came as a surprise to me to realise that when God gives a prophecy he gives a general sense, or a general feeling. He does not give the individual words. I had expected that God might put a spiritual video screen into my head so that when I saw a word flash up on the screen I would read it off!

Often I would go to a meeting and have a real feeling inside that something specific needed to be said. I never realised that prophecy is simply a matter of my putting those specific feelings into my own words and communicating the heart of what God is wanting to say. Now I understand that all God is looking for in prophecy is a person who is willing to speak out things which he is wanting to say!

2. *I am the channel*
When I was wanting to step out in prophecy I used to go to many meetings where prophecies would be given. Sometimes these would be by way of a picture someone would see rather than words. Often these prophecies would be given by middle-aged ladies who had time on their hands during the day to read their Bibles, pray and become really spiritual! The pictures would be of rolling hillsides, gentle lambs skipping down lush green turf into the arms of a smiling shepherd dressed in white! I would sit there and think, "Lord, I cannot imagine ever getting a prophecy like that!"

Often prophecy was given in seventeenth-century language. The interesting thing was that after the meeting the same people would turn round and say, "Hi, Rich, how's it all going, mate. Everything okay, pal?'' For prophecy we would slip into our best evangelical accents but for ''real'' chatting we would revert to our normal way of talking!

Similarly people used to think that a prophecy would sound a whole lot better and would add a real authority to what is said (especially if the giver was not too sure about it!) by keeping on slipping in those immortal words ''Thus saith the Lord''. Actually I got to the point where I began to think that if the person giving the prophecy had to keep slipping those little words in, he was probably not too sure that the content was really from God anyway!

Prophecy should speak for itself. If it is powerful you do not need to keep saying it is from God. Everyone will know that it is. If it is not really from God then merely adding those words will not suddenly transform it and make it from God!

It is important that we teach children to be natural. They can so easily be put off because they look at the externals when they hear others giving prophecies and feel that their humble little offering could never match up. I remember once praying for a couple with marriage difficulties. After praying with them I began to prophesy over them. I knew the basic message was that things will not always be easy and that sometimes it will be hard work. In the event I said that things will not always be easy and that sometimes it will be hard graft. Then I stopped and asked myself the question: Does God say ''hard graft''? Immediately I realised that God was simply using my own way of speaking to convey what he actually wanted to say into that situation. I felt not only relieved but humbled to think that Almighty God is happy to communicate in the way that the people he chooses to use happen to be!

3. *The possibility of error*
Because prophecy is all about me speaking out what I *believe*

God wants to say, there is always room for error. It might be me rather than God!

The fact is that it is very rare for a prophecy to be all of God or all of me. The reality is that especially at the beginning it will be part God and part me. The basic idea will normally be from God, but often in the giving out of the message a bit of me will creep in as well. I found that once I had launched out into prophecy the problem was knowing where to stop!

With children especially we need to provide a safe environment where prophecy can be practised and where if mistakes are made they are protected, or covered, by the leaders. After all, we all make mistakes! It is surely better to step out in faith and go for it even if one or two mistakes are made, than to clam up and stay quiet for fear of making a mistake. It is the job of the church to weigh what is brought, it is not the job of the person giving the prophecy to bring it and weigh it. If any serious errors are made, leaders will always be present to put things right.

Making it easy for children
Prophecy needs to be made simple for children. This can in fact be done quite easily. It is often helpful to remind them how they learned to draw. They started off joining the dots to make a picture. Similarly when they learned to paint they started off by painting by numbers. This illustration helps to explain that God too has a way of making prophecy easy for us when we start. It is called prophecy by picture.

Once the children are happily worshipping in tongues it is good to explain a little about what prophecy means and tell them to ask God for a picture.

In larger meetings I normally have a leader at the front to check out the pictures with the children. Then they come up onto the stage and tell everyone what they saw. As soon as one or two have started it generally leads to more. Often one ends up with more pictures than the Tate Gallery!

Very often the pictures speak to someone specific. Sometimes they are general. Occasionally one can hardly make head or tail of the picture in the first place. That is fine. The children have made a start. The gift simply needs a chance to develop.

There was a time when these pictures were called "visions". This rather grand term is less popular now. It does not really matter what we call them provided the children understand the basic concept. Asking children to "share a prophetic vision God had just laid on your heart" may not be quite so readily understandable as asking them to "tell us about the picture you saw in your head when you asked God for it".

Words of knowledge

Once someone has got going in prophecy, the other gifts come very naturally. In fact there is quite an overlap between the various gifts. The way in which one receives a prophecy is very similar to the way one receives a word of knowledge.

A word of knowledge is simply inside information given by God relating to a person or situation.

I have sometimes glanced around at the front of a meeting and known little things about people to the extent where I could have picked them out and told them what was going on inside their lives.

With children words of knowledge can be explained as an extension of prophecy. It is God giving you a general sense of what he wants to say to a particular individual or in a particular situation. Again it could be by picture, by general "feeling" or—especially with healing—by physical sensation.

I once asked a boy to come onto the stage who had responded after some teaching on words of knowledge. I asked his name and found his age was nine. When I asked what he felt God wanted to say he seemed quite definite. He said there was a girl present whose parents were always fighting and arguing and were heading for divorce, and who was feeling very sad and upset. I stood on the stage rigid. This was either spot on or a potential disaster! In the event a young girl stood up, tears streaming down her face. I got the two of them together with a leader to pray the issue through.

On another occasion a young boy had a word of knowledge that someone had something wrong with his left knee. There followed what every leader dreads. Silence! The boy was quite sure about it but still there was no response. I asked him whether it was a boy or girl and he said it was a boy. Still there was no response. I asked him his age which he gave me, but still no response. Then I asked him to wander round and find him whilst we carried on. I was hoping that would be the last we heard of it! Suddenly after a few minutes he called out, "I've found him!" I could hardly believe it. Sure enough there was the boy with a damaged left knee!

Many stories could be told but the important point to grasp is this. Children really do have the capacity to be used in words of knowledge and we need to be encouraging this in the Church.

Interpretation of tongues
Once again it is true to say that once prophecy has been grasped, interpretation of tongues will come naturally.

An interpretation is very different from a translation. When I was in Poland recently I spoke in English—not being able to speak Polish! Every sentence I spoke was translated into Polish so that people could understand what I was saying. However, an interpretation of a tongue is not the translation. It is the general feeling behind what has been said by the person who has just given the tongue. The interpretation, being a general sense, will come out in the style that the person interpreting would ordinarily use. Again there is nothing spiritual in using traditional evangelical jargon to add authenticity!

Once I was able to speak in tongues I would dread someone in the meeting giving a public tongue. I knew that the Bible tells us to pray for the interpretation and I was nervous about doing this—in case I actually got the interpretation. Then I would have to speak it out and it might be wrong. People might think less of me, I reasoned. So I tended not to bother to pray, preferring to stay with the familiarity of mediocrity rather than take any risks! Here again we need to be prepared to step out ourselves and to encourage our children to do the same.

There is an interesting theological point about interpretation of tongues that we need to think through carefully as it may affect how we teach the gift to children. It could be argued that when we speak in tongues, whether personally or as a public tongue in a meeting, it is us speaking out to God. The essence of tongues is that it is our spirit communicating with God. Tongues is therefore a cry from the heart in an "upward" direction, i.e. from us to God. On the other hand, the argument goes, a prophecy is not us speaking to God but rather God speaking in a "downward" direction, to us.

If this is correct we would expect an interpretation to be in the first person: me expressing my love to God and my feelings for him, perhaps my frustrations and so on. An interpretation would not therefore be God speaking to us, it would be us speaking to God. The argument states, quite logically, that if interpretations are "downward" rather than "upward" there is no point having them because they are no different from prophecies.

Experience shows that most tongues are in practice interpreted as God speaking to us rather than as my heart being poured out to God. Are these wrong? What is the correct answer to all this?

I would not want to be too dogmatic about it. Certainly I would not want to discourage anyone in any way from using the gifts. As an individual I tend towards thinking that the argument outlined above is correct. When an interpretation is given that is expressed as being from God to us, it is not wrong. It is more likely simply to be a prophecy rather than an interpretation! In any event we should not become too steamed up over it because in some ways it does not matter what we call the gifts provided we are exercising them. If this view is correct, it means that for many years we have perhaps not seen very many true interpretations of tongues, we have more likely "interpreted" with a prophecy from God.

To me there is a much greater richness in seeing interpretations in this light. When a tongue is interpreted the whole church will be able to understand an individual's heart cry to God (in addition to prophecies) which can be very moving indeed and can even be a turning point in a meeting, leading to deeper worship.

Other gifts
The aim of this part of the book is to consider how to get the children going with the gifts of the Spirit. It is not designed as an all-embracing encyclopedia on the subject. If the children can become experienced in tongues, prophecy, words of knowledge and interpretations, they will be off to a very good start.

Some of the other gifts, notably faith and healing, will be covered as separate topics in their own right in later chapters. Discernment of spirits is perhaps not an area where we would normally want to involve children whilst they are still on the nursery slopes in the Spirit. It will sometimes happen that a child may sense something specific which is causing a problem in a particular situation. If this happens it needs to be treated like a word of knowledge and acted upon—but not by the child. Deliverance is an important subject but one that can lead to difficulties if children are thrown into it too early without those around them really knowing what they are doing themselves.

Realising the potential

When I was leading a weekend away for the children of one fellowship, on the Saturday evening most of them were worshipping in tongues and were prophesying. One boy really sticks out in my memory. He was aged eleven and suffered from dyslexia. He started giving prophecies and as usual I encouraged the leaders to keep it all going back in the home church. A few months later I heard that the boy had been regularly used in prophecy in the main church meetings. Also, and this still amazes me, he went with his Mum and Dad when they were involved in a week's ministry at another church. Close to the beginning this little lad got up and began to prophesy in that meeting also. It was so powerful that it actually changed the whole direction of the week's ministry and many people experienced the touch of God in a powerful way. His Dad told me that their family life had also been revolutionised!

As well as being an enormous personal encouragement, this confirmed to me the strategic place children have in the Kingdom. Children can be used by God in amazing ways. It all starts by moving on from the basics and seeing our youngsters securely led into the gifts of the Holy Spirit whilst they are still children.

Chapter 8

Children and the Holy Spirit – Checks and Balances

No car manufacturer would find a car with an engine but no brakes. The potential for disaster is only too obvious. It is one thing to be able to race away, but a release of power and energy needs to be channelled. This is not simply to avoid disaster but more particularly to ensure that the vehicle is able to operate safely and to achieve the purpose for which it was designed. So too with the power of the Holy Spirit.

I have met many people who have had bad experiences when it comes to the gifts of the Holy Spirit, and especially prophecy. They have been left disillusioned. What is worse, they have rejected spiritual renewal on the basis of their own unfortunate experiences and have thrown the baby out with the bathwater.

I once led a seminar in a Methodist church on a Saturday evening. At the end of the evening I began to pray for people. This led (rather unusually at a seminar) to my moving round from person to person prophesying over them. Later on, back at the organiser's house, I was told that the whole group had suffered a very bad experience with someone over the issue of the Holy Spirit. That night God had used the words he gave me to restore their confidence in renewal in general and in the gift of the Spirit in particular.

The emphasis on the Holy Spirit in recent years has been like a torrent of water that had risen. It is as though the floodgates have been opened and the banks of the river have overflowed. Water everywhere! As the flood begins to subside following the initial rush of water we are left with a much more controlled flow. Of course the river is flowing faster now than it did before because it is holding more water.

The problem is that there will always be a few puddles on each bank which represent some extreme movement that has somehow got lost, missed its way, failed to be joined to the main flow of the river and been left isolated.

All of this, of course, has been in the adult world of the church. When it comes to seeing children filled with the Holy Spirit it becomes even more important to realise that God has provided us with checks and balances. Whilst we need to see children encouraged in the gifts, we need to be aware of the dangers. It is up to us to provide guidance, set safe limits and recognise any warning signs, so that we can see God's power channelled positively and constructively. The last thing any of us wants is a trail of disaster left behind as our children steam full speed down blind alleys.

Giving Guidelines for the use of the gifts
The possibility of abuse is as real with young people as it is with adults. As leader it is our responsibility to be alert and to be aware of any potential problems. The two most common areas of abuse are as follows:

1. *Attention seeking*
Sometimes people can purport to prophesy or give what is claimed to be a world of knowledge because they want the limelight. At one recent national conference there was a boy of twelve in our meetings who constantly wanted to be in the spotlight. Unfortunately he tried to get everyone's attention by claiming to have a prophecy so that he could stand at the front and be seen. We had observed this lad in the meeting and had the clear impression that all was not well long before we began to teach on the Holy Spirit.

In this case, as with all other "major meeting" situations, I insisted that any prophecy, word of knowledge, interpretation and so on was checked out with one of my leaders before we let a child loose on stage with a microphone, under a spotlight. A specific system of checking is vital in this context.

In the slightly more straightforward local church scene where the leaders will know the children, things are a little easier but still there need to be checks. In a small group situation leaders will know those who are seeking recognition and will therefore be able to deal with the situation more easily.

In all this leader do need to be sensitive. It just may be that the extrovert attention-seeker will actually have a genuine word from God! This highlights the crucial distinction between gifting on the one hand and character on the other. This will be looked at in slightly more detail later in this chapter.

2. Manipulation

The possibility of using the gifts as a cloak of spirituality to control and manipulate others will always be with us. It is perhaps less likely with children and young people than with adults but we certainly need to be aware of it. The object of prophecy especially is to build up no tear down, to accentuate the positive not dwell on the negative, to encourage not condemn. Sometimes "prophecy" can be all gloom and doom, heavy and harsh, having the effect of depressing and belittling God's people. It is always worth remembering that the Holy Spirit is the comforter not the accuser. Obviously there are times when correction and order are needed but we must always be aware of those who will try to use the gifts to further their own ends, to put the church right, to "correct" the leadership and so on.

When considering potential abuse of the gifts we need

to keep a sense of perspective. There will always be the potential for abuse but in my experience it is quite rare with children and young people. If we over-emphasise abuse we are likely to discourage children from receiving from God and giving out what they receive. Abuse is something leaders need to be aware of but not something which needs to be taught to and laboured with children. Clearly those individual children who may on rare occasions seem to be getting close to the mark need to be taken on one side for some friendly advice.

One very practical area we need to be aware of when encouraging people in the gifts is the possibility of interpreting and applying what we receive. This is true of children as well as adults. Sometimes a prophetic word, for example, may be very short. If we give a very short word the temptation is to want to put flesh on the bones and to try to interpret it. I have often found that one short word of prophecy perhaps only a sentence, can speak to two people very specifically, but in very different ways. Any attempt at elaboration would have been superfluous and, even worse, would have actually detracted from what God wants to say.

Teaching discernment
Giving out one of the gifts of the Spirit is like one side of a coin. The other side, which is equally important, is how we *receive* what is given. There are several important guidelines we need to bear in mind on the whole question of receiving and understanding what is given.

1. Weighing it
Although it is the responsibility of the individual to give what he or she believes God wants to say, it is a corporate responsibility to weigh it. This is especially true of prophecy. In a children's context the same principle applies. If the gifts are used in a specific children-only meeting it means in

practice that it is part of the leader's responsibility to weigh what is brought.

Weighing is often thought of in the context of deciding whether it was right or not, i.e. whether it was truly from God. However, weighing means more than that. The leader should be able to weigh up the way the word was brought, the time it was brought as well as the content of the word itself. A few minutes spent talking over these issues quietly with the giver in a friendly way will actually help to encourage that person's development and progress in the use of the gifts.

Sometimes what is brought as a "gift of the Spirit" can be bland. The content is not wrong but somehow does not really say anything. In this kind of case one does not want to say, when weighing it, that it was wrong and should be rejected. But we may wish to get alongside that child to encourage a more specific or direct content as time goes on.

I would never reject what purports to be a spiritual gift publicly unless it is against scripture and clearly wrong. There have been times when I have done this but it has been very rare indeed. More commonly I have found it necessary to step in and give a little bit of direction, But this operates not as a rejection of what is brought but as an encouragement and a shaping.

One very important point about weighing is that this is only possible when words are given in a public context. When someone takes another person aside after the meeting and begins to speak into that person's life in private, it cannot be weighed because there is no opportunity. This is, generally speaking, a bad practice and not to be encouraged. Prophecy, especially, needs to be weighed. I always ask children to speak in a "public" context and will do the same myself. Sometimes it does happen that a personal word is given. That is fine provided it is then shared with and checked out with that person's leaders. What I am very much against is private prophecy given privately by some free-wheeling, lone-ranger person who is unaccountable uncontrollable and invisible!

2. *Understanding it*

Words which apply to some future time may not be readily understood now, because they refer to a different time. When faced with this I have put such words to the side of my plate until the time is right for me to be able to receive them. It is not that the word is wrong – it may just take time to work out.

I once prophesied over a young girl that she would be used by God internationally. Her parents and leaders were at the meeting and so were able to weigh it. In many ways the prophecy could not make too much sense to her just now as she is still at school! But the time will come when the way will open up for her in the future.

It is therefore important that, having weighed such words, we hold on to them. I have adopted a practice of writing down prophecies people give me in the front of my main diary so that I have a record of what was said, who said it, and when it was said. This is a great way of holding on to what God has said and praying over the fulfilment.

It is always good to share prophecies we have received, especially with our leaders. We as leaders must be prepared to stand with our children on these things and pray with them to see the fulfilment. Opening these words up to the fellowship brings in visibility and accountability. Things are much less likely to go wrong when everything is out in the open.

It is always worth bearing in mind that the gifts are like one piece in a bigger jigsaw. They are a part of the overall picture, not the picture itself. Children will need to understand that there are other pieces to the jigsaw that will need to be attended to as well. Whilst it is always good to pray and work towards the fulfilment of prophetic words, we should try not to burn ourselves out wanting to see it all happen right now and feeling desperately frustrated when it does not seem to work out quite as quickly as we would like.

Character and gifting

As we have seen in the context of developing children's ministries, there is a wealth of difference between character and gifting. Unfortunately we tend not to recognise this crucial distinction in the context of spiritual gifts. A person may be very gifted, there may be frequent use of the gift of the Spirit, but if that same person's character is weak and underdeveloped there will be trouble.

Gifting needs to run side by side with character. The integrity of the Kingdom of God is at stake. An unreliable person, doing his own thing and prophesying over people, could easily be a recipe for disaster.

Discerning and weighing words that are given is much easier if the person giving them is known to be reliable, mature and trustworthy. Although these tend to be thought of as adult traits, children do possess these qualities albeit in a slightly less developed form. As we build character and see the fruits of the Spirit developing in our children we will automatically create an environment in which the gifts can be exercised in safety and with security.

Chapter 9

Reaching the Whole Person

We are all products not only of our own characters and personalities but also of our experiences. We are as we are today, as individuals, to a large extent because of the people and situations we have been involved with in the past.

Much of this may have been positive. Perhaps, for example, we were discipled, either formally or informally, by good friends when we were new Christians. Perhaps we have been involved in churches where we have been able to grown and develop. Maybe a conference has given inspiration, and a one-off meeting, a book, tape or video has changed our perception and helped shape our views and experience of God.

By the same token we know that other things also have shaped our lives. In some cases, particularly where there has been involvement in the occult, people have been seriously damaged. In less serious cases there are many of us who are affected in the present by things of the past. The fact is that unless these things are dealt with they will continue to affect us. They will not mysteriously go away. Our whole future potential can be sapped by these same old past issues.

Almost everywhere I go I notice that many children are already suffering from the effects of past experiences. If we are looking to see the church equipped with people who are coming to wholeness in Christ, we cannot view this vital area as an adult-only issue. I could write a whole book on experiences I have had praying for children with real fears, deep hurt, rejection, inferiorities and many other problems. We cannot afford to sweep this vital area under the carpet.

We must face the issues head on and see the power of God heal and set our children free. Obviously this applies to adults as well.

I once went in to Dartmoor prison to lead a meeting and to talk with the prisoners. During my session with them I managed to pluck up the courage to say something I felt was significant – before making a dash for it while the going was good! I reminded the inmates that they were in prison because of what they had done in the past. I explained how the past was having a direct bearing on their lives in the present. I went on to say that in the future when they were released (most of them!) they might find it difficult to get a job. This is not because they are not capable of working – far from it. It is because the issues of the past will inevitably affect their future as well. On this particular occasion I went on to explain that Jesus has the power to forgive and forget, to set our clock back to zero so that we can start all over again with a brand new life that God will help us lead by the power of the Holy Spirit.

The irony for us as Christians, of whatever age, is that there are many of us who know all about new life in Jesus, have perhaps been Christians for years and yet are still bound up with issues from the past. Often at meetings I can stand at the front and pick out those suffering in this way. It is written all over their faces. It is in their body language. They appear to be living in defeat and usually look closed up and depressed, looking down at floor.

So what is the answer? We all know the answer. The problem is getting into the reality of the fact that Jesus is the answer.

The needs of young people can be particularly acute. After a recent youth meeting a girl of sixteen asked me to pray for her addiction to alcohol. Another asked me to pray for the result of sexual abuse she suffered as a child. I have been asked to pray with many whose problems have included drugs and the occult. However, the need is not just with young people. Recently I prayed with an older man who is a young Christian and who still suffers from the effects of abuse from his father which took place when he was a boy. Many adults in our churches are completely bound up from such experiences and need to be released.

When it comes to children it seems there is no less work to do. I have prayed for literally hundreds of children whose problems have not always been so dramatic but are equally real.

Sometimes they have been hurt by people and find it difficult to trust others, especially adults. Often children think they are worthless, useless, can do nothing and are inferior. Sometimes they feel rejected, they feel that no one understands them or loves them just the way they are. Then there are the insecure children, those who constantly demand attention and try to make an impact because no one at home can be bothered with them. And these are all children within the church.

Christians would all agree that the answer to all these problems is Jesus. Yet if we are not careful this can sound trite and theoretical. The time has come to stop giving pat Christian answers. Somehow we must find a way of grounding this basic truth into the reality of the children's lives right where they are. I have found that this starts with an understanding of the fatherhood of God.

God is my Father

I had been a Christian for years. I knew all about Jesus being my Saviour. I was learning all about the Holy Spirit and the power of God. But I had hardly any concept of God as my Father. This may have been due in part do my own experience with my human father. It was also the result of an almost total lack of teaching about the fatherhood of God.

More recently I have discovered an amazing theological concept which I have never heard preached on. I mean the following statement with real reverence. It is simply this:

"God is nice and he likes me." We all know that God is love. But what on earth does this really mean in my own life? I have found a new release as I have meditated on these words: "God is nice and he likes me."

Although we know that God is love, we sometimes think that God is not nice and that at best we are tolerated by him rather than truly accepted by him. Many of our children and young people have exactly this concept of God and of themselves.

I once led a session for inner-city children and youth in London. I asked them to do a very simple exercise to find out their real concept of God. I gave them all a piece of A4 paper and got them to draw a picture of God *and* a picture of themselves on one side of the paper.

The results amazed me. Naturally there were some who drew what they thought I wanted to see – which was great if it really summed up their own true feelings. Some drawings however were very sad. One lad showed me his drawing which made me want to cry. It showed God, large and overbearing, in the top right hand corner. In his hand was a club-like object. God was seen as remote and far away, ready to punish anything wrong. The picture of himself on the same page was drawn as far away as it is possible to get, in the diagonally opposite corner. He showed himself as being small and insignificant, distanced from God and worthless. What an image of both God and self!

It turned out that the little guy came from a broken home. It was also very obvious that no one had ever sat down next to him and showed him God as a Father. As Adrian Plass says, we so often see God as a cross between a headmaster and a bank manager and ourselves as naughty little schoolchildren with a horrendous overdraft!

We need to show our children that God is nice and that he likes us. We need to show them that God is on our side as well as that we are on his side. We need to teach them that he wants the best for us. Some of us have to be prepared to come through the hoop first and receive ministry ourselves before we can then see our children's lives changed.

Problems, Problems, Problems . . .

Once we fully grasp that God is on our side and wants the best for us, we can then start to unscramble some of the individual issues in our lives. For many of us, including our children, our lives can be like plates of spaghetti with many complex strands. It can take time to untangle the mess.

It is always important, especially with children, never to be "heavy". One thing that I find irritating is when people are asked to dig deeply into their lives to drag up something that needs to be healed. I am not a believer in deep sea fishing in this context. My experience is that important issues tend to float to the surface and become obvious.

Many are familiar with house group meetings where everyone is busy sharing their problems. There is, of course, a place for this. But often I have gone along to a meeting happy and cheerful and come home feeling depressed and miserable! What is worse, if one quite genuinely has no particular problem this week one begins to feel guilty and unspiritual! You suspect people feel you had problems really but needed prayer to be able to share them in the group. Before you know where you are you have been psychoanalysed by well-meaning friends and feel you must dredge up something just to keep up with the Joneses!

I can remember in the days when I worked in an office I would (as well as getting the work done) have a good laugh with my non-Christian colleagues. We would have good chats and play snooker at lunchtimes. The relationships were light and happy. The problem was that I would get home and then go to housegroup. Sometimes the atmosphere there would be intense. People would not always be relaxed. Then we would share all our problems. It used to strike me as quite interesting to compare the way

119

we related to each other with the way I related to non-Christian friends. I began to realise that with all the emphasis on "relationships" we had almost totally by-passed ordinary friendship! We chose to be heavy and "spiritual" in the way we tried to share our problems.

Problems are there to be solved. Yet I have met many people who do not want to be helped out of their problems at all. Sometimes we even build up a certain security in our problems, hanging on to them so that we have a legitimate excuse for why we are not maturing in our lives. It is possible to enjoy being the centre of attention and receiving a lot of sympathy so much that we do not really want to be free of the things we keep talking about.

Once whilst praying for someone I had a picture of a person carrying a large, heavy sack to Jesus who was on the cross. As the lady approached Jesus she put her sack down as she looked him in the face and received from him. Then as she turned to go she nearly forgot her sack. So she stopped, picked it back up again and went on her way. The interpretation is obvious. I believe this is not an uncommon response. We can get so used to carrying our heavy load that we do not feel right without it and so choose to pick it up again.

God want his people whole. Yet so often we seem to spend time with the same people going over the same old ground time and time again. We are not called to be a problem-centred people. These issues need to be dealt with if we are going to make real progress.

Our children will take the lead from us. If they perceive that the Kingdom of God is only about talking through our problems, they will soon feel the need to get something to talk about!

Fears

One of the most common problems I have come across in children as well as adults is fear. With children it can be fear of death, parents separating, illness, fire, dark, spiders, school and so on. They may seem trivial to adults (just as adults' fears may seem trivial to God!) but they are real fears as far as the children are concerned. I once prayed for a girl at a weekend away in Scarborough who had a real fear connected with her school. This little one was close to tears and I could tell that it was an important issue as far as she was concerned and needed to be taken seriously.

Fear is a serious issue because it is the antithesis of faith. Fear and faith are like oil and water. If children know only fear they will find it difficult to take steps of faith and see God meeting with them in a way which goes beyond the normal. God needs to be seen as able and willing to deal with real issues. If we cannot see fears overcome it is unlikely that we will see any significant breakthroughs taking place in other areas.

Hurts

We all get hurt from time to time. It is as inevitable as falling over in a playground. What I have noticed though is that our recovery times seem to vary enormously. Sometimes adults hold on to hurts for years on end, never trying to get them sorted out with the person who first hurt them. I have even seen cases where the original issues have been lost but the hurt remains and no one is quite sure why!

In a playground some children who fall over and get hurt will pick themselves up, brush themselves down and carry on. Others (like me!) will make a fuss, start to limp, pretend it is much worse than it really is and demand first aid, sympathy, attention and possibly a teacher! It is not the hurt but the recovery time that is important.

Whilst it is true to say that as individuals we should not give offence, it is also true that we should not take offence. Just today I received a letter from a church I visited to say that what I did was not particularly accepted and that there had been complaints. Being fairly sensitive I could easily be hurt by that as I did everything openly, checked everything out with the leaders beforehand and did everything before the Lord. I knew I had to take action. Lynda and I prayed together for our own attitudes to be right and for the church concerned to be blessed!

People will let us down. We should be ready to deal with our responses when this occurs. People can choose to make a real meal out of hurts, making a drama out of a crisis. They are then excused for not getting stuck in to Kingdom life because they have been "hurt". The result is that our churches can become like hospital wards rather than battle stations!

If our children see long-term unresolved hurts in our own lives they will accept it as a normal part of Kingdom living. We must overcome hurts. We must ask the forgiveness of others involved and then carry on with the job in hand. We owe it to our children in the interests of seeing secure spiritual foundations being built into their lives. Also we need to be in a position to minister effectively into their lives.

Rejection and insecurity

Rejection and insecurity often go together. An insecure person is likely to have suffered real or perceived rejection at some stage, which caused them hurt and pain. I have lived through this and know exactly how it feels.

As a teenager in a Christian home I had somehow to come to terms with the fact that my Dad's heavy drinking was tearing our family apart. I would sometimes literally cry myself to sleep and would ask God why all this had to happen to us in general and me in particular. On the outside everything appeared normal in our family life. On the inside everything was falling apart. I found that I was becoming very insecure and wanted to keep everyone at a nice safe distance. I did not want anyone coming too close to me in case they saw the real me. I did not want to run the risk of shattering the illusion and then finding people rejecting me. Looking back, this kind of thinking is perhaps irrational, but it is how I felt at the time.

As I write this I can feel my heart beating faster as I relive it all in my mind. It had a profound effect on me which only prayer – and time – has healed. Just five years ago I could never have shared this with anyone let alone write it down for all to read. Even now I still feel I have a scar where all the hurt has been and would like to be completely healed of insecurity.

My own experience has taught me valuable lessons. Whilst I will always pray with children (and adults) for healing of hurts, fears, bad memories and so on I believe it is important not to pray quick, cheap, wham-bam type prayers. The issues which God deals with over a period of time are the ones which generally result in the most lasting healing. The short, sharp "everything-is-fine-now" prayers seem to achieve very little in the long term.

I have found it good to pray specifically into the area of need. I generally ask God to break hold of the root cause of the problem, cut off the past, and pray for the Holy Spirit to fill the gap. Then I believe it is important for these people to receive ongoing support from their church and be supported by praying friends so that a full healing can be worked into their lives. It is important to use the gifts of the Spirit to identify the real areas of need. A word of knowledge can be vital in understanding the real root cause. Often the issue put forward by the person being prayed for is not the real issue at all.

Deliverance

In looking at issues such as fears, hurts, rejections and so on it is important that we recognise the games Satan plays and understand the need for deliverance.

Deliverance is a huge subject in itself. It is usually met with a mixture of fright and caution. When dealing with children we would not normally see deliverance as having any application.

Before we talk about it in relation to children we need to know what we are talking about. I am certainly no expert but I hope my own experience will help to bring the whole issue down to earth.

I was sitting in a café with a friend after the end of an evening session at a national Bible week. We were minding our own business drinking a cup of tea when suddenly the door opened and a lady burst through in what can only be described as something of a panic. Our table happened to be nearest the door and so she approached us. "Quick!" she pleaded, "You've got to come!" I never like leaving a cup of tea half drunk but on this occasion I had to be self-sacrificing! The lady explained to us that a young man in her party was busy tearing up phone books and was about to vandalise the phone box. Horror stories came out about irrational behaviour, criminal damage and demonic activity. I tried to keep calm and look cool but really I was quite nervous wondering what if . . . Anyway the young man wanted to be prayed for and so we met with him and started praying for him. As we did so we began to ask God what to do.

Gradually by a series of pictures and words of knowledge we were shown the root cause of the underlying problems which included homosexuality. All we did was bind the spiritual forces affecting him as specifically as we could and tell him to go home to bed.

Some people think deliverance always involves frothing at the mouth, people rolling on the floor, maniacal laughter and so on. Although these things do happen they are only the dramatic tip of the deliverance iceberg. There is so much more to it. And the good news is that any Spirit-filled Christian can deal with it. You do not have to send away for the special Man with the Ministry!

In times past we made heavy weather of the fine-line

distinction between oppression and possession. Some people were troubled at the doctrinal possibility that a Christian could have a demon. So to fit in with what was seen to be an ugly concept someone came up with the idea that a Christian could not be "possessed" but could only be "oppressed". I have never been very satisfied with this distinction. It has always seemed a little artificial. As I have thought it through, an alternative view has suggested itself to me which I find far more convincing.

Demonic influence is, I believe, not Yes or No, black or white. Rather it is on a sliding scale from zero to infinity. A Christian can be affected to varying degrees. It is not a matter of possession, it is a matter of recognising the degree to which one has been affected and getting rid of that influence. It is similar with spiritual maturity. It is not a question of being "holy" or "unspiritual", to use the same analogy, rather it is a question of how far along the scale we have come.

Let me put it into concrete terms. When I was closed up and hurt in my own life, it meant that Satan had something of a foothold. I needed to recognise this and have his influence prayed out. It was not a question of possession or oppression, it was a case of being set free from the degree of influence over my life. By contrast, the man we had to abandon our cups of tea for and pray with was clearly being influenced and affected at a much more serious level. But Jesus was equally able to set him free as well as me.

In all this what we are talking about is deliverance. It is not necessarily the way we have traditionally understood the term, but it is deliverance from the effect of Satan's grip on our lives.

In talking about deliverance we must not run away with the idea that there is a full-blown demon under every bed! Some have gone overboard on this and have become somewhat unbalanced. A good friend of mine recently attended a seminar in the Midlands on deliverance. During the afternoon all the delegates were asked to stand in groups of two, place hands on their partner's shoulders and pray. My friend could feel a sneeze coming on and he knew instinctively what was going to happen! As the inevitable happened his partner said, "That's right, let it come out," as though somehow demons would be expelled in the sneeze! I know that in certain circumstances demons will be cast out in a sneeze but this was a case of a sneeze pure and simple!

If we accept that Satan's influence is on a sliding scale it will come as no surprise that most "deliverance" will not be the dramatic fireworks display that some expect. In fact one would expect the fireworks only in the most extreme cases. Most deliverance will be much more down to earth and low key, and operates in the realm of fears, rejections, insecurities and other similar issues.

As with other spiritual areas, we learn from experience. Fear of mistakes should not prevent us from stepping out. But I have to confess to an embarrassing incident last year. I was driving over Salisbury Plain late at night on Hallowe'en. As I drove along I could see bonfires and was aware that this was a witches' stronghold. Driving up a hill I saw a large amber glow and decided that I would not put up with all this nonsense. I wound my window down, stretched out my arm and began to rebuke it in the name of Jesus. It was only as I reached the top of the hill I realised to my surprise that I had actually rebuked an amber street lamp which was glowing on an adjacent road!

Lazarus

What we have been dealing with in this chapter is very neatly illustrated in the life (or, rather, death) of Lazarus (John 11).

Mary, Martha and Lazarus were family friends of Jesus. They were very ordinary people who lived in Bethany which was a couple of miles outside the capital, Jerusalem. Life was fine except that Lazarus was not feeling too good. As time went on he got worse until his sisters were starting to get worried about him. No doubt they did everything possible from a medical point of view but nothing seemed to work. They became desperate.

As Jesus was a family friend it made sense to ask him to do something. But Jesus was away in the north of the country. When the message reached him Jesus simply carried on with what he was doing. Two days later he made the journey down to Bethany with his disciples.

When Jesus arrived one can just imagine the scene. Mourners were around, the atmosphere was heavy and as Jesus approached the house he was met by Mary and Martha, grieving for Lazarus who had died.

When Martha met Jesus she said something very interesting. One can almost feel the hurt in her voice when she turned to Jesus and said, "Lord, if you had been here, my brother would not have died." Jesus told her that Lazarus would rise again but Martha's response showed exactly where her faith was. She said in effect that she knew everything would be all right in the next life. But that was not what Jesus was saying. He said, "I *am* the resurrection and the life."

Martha was not ignorant. She would have known her Old Testament. She would have been able to look back to a time when God was in the healing business. She would for example have been familiar with the accounts of people like Elijah and Elisha who had ministries of signs and wonders in the Old Testament.

Martha as a personal friend of Jesus also knew that he was doing great things in her own day. Jesus was healing the sick, delivering from demons, preaching with authority, showing compassion, yet all these things were taking place with other people in other places. What she was not able to accept was that God could actually intervene in her own real life situation in the here-and-now.

127

Jesus approached the tomb. The stone was taken away and he gave a simple word of command, "Lazarus, come forth!" Lazarus, who had been dead four days and whose body was beginning to rot, began to move. He got up and came out. It was a miracle which only Jesus could have done.

When Lazarus emerged, there was a serious problem. Although he was now alive again, which was a miracle, he was bound hand and foot with graveclothes. He was alive – but bound up! Jesus then turned to those who were with him and said to *them*, "Loose him and let him go." Although Jesus could easily have unbound him he chose to involve his own people in the process and, at God's command, they were able to set him free.

What an amazing incident! The point is that although Lazarus had been raised to new life, he was bound by the clothes of death. With fears, hurts, insecurities and so on we can similarly be bound up. To be released we may have to swallow our pride and ask someone to pray for us so that we can begin the process of release in our lives.

It is true also that like Martha some of us do not believe that Jesus will do anything. Of course we all believe that he *could* do it but we really do not believe it will actually happen in our own situation. We know it will all be all right in the next life. We know that Jesus used to heal in Bible times. We even know (through books, tapes and videos) that God is doing it today – with other people, somewhere else. The question is: what about us? Are we going to reach out to Jesus knowing that he is "I am" (present tense) and see ourselves beginning to be released from our own fears, hurts, rejections and so on?

If we really believe that our children need to come through on some of these issues it is going to require people like you and me to make it happen. We need to be there first so that we can minister effectively to our children.

It is important to recognise that as Christians we are not called to psychology. But we are called to healing.

Sometimes as leaders we can fancy ourselves as amateur psychologists as we try to analyse situations and people. But we are called not to identify problems but to provide solutions. By asking God to reveal the root of issues by his Spirit, and by seeing deliverance from demonic influence, we shall see the Kingdom becoming more strongly established among the whole church family in our local situation.

Chapter 10

Developing Children's Ministries

Over the past few years there has been an emphasis on gifts and ministries in church teaching. People are seen not as passive individuals who dutifully turn up to church to have their ears tickled. Instead we have rediscovered that church is a living body of people that we are part of, rather than a dead institution we go to. Everyone has a place, a role, a ministry, something they can do. The emphasis on ministries, and seeing those ministries released, has been good. It is part of the impact the Holy Spirit has created in bringing in renewal and restoration. The only question is: What about our children?

As we have already seen, children are people too! As Christians they are every bit as much part of the Church as we are. It follows that we must expect to see ministries being developed in their lives also. Otherwise we are saying that a person can only have a ministry when he or she has reached some sort of qualifying age!

I have discovered in my travels that many adults do not have a clue as to what God has specifically called us to do. We seem to be content to lurch on from week to week, month to month and year to year without really knowing where our lives are going. All this talk about ministries is too complex, it is all beyond us. We recognise people with "real" ministries but we are not like them, never will be and therefore cannot have a valid ministry.

If this is how we think, how on earth shall we be able to encourage our children into their own ministries? First of all we must deal with these issues in our own lives. Only then will we be in a position to lead our children in a way that will not be cold and theoretical.

An example of this occurred recently. Whilst leading an all-age celebration in Wales I was able to pray with a man whom God had called into full-time ministry. I knew nothing about anyone in the meeting, but this came out by word of knowledge. He was encouraged and so was I. It was great to see the way God was at work revealing his plans for our lives at meetings which were for children, too. Our children will respect us more, not less, if they see us responding to God in meetings!

Ministries, gifts and talents
Ministries must be distinguished from talents. A talent is a God-given natural ability. Talents need to be positively encouraged within the Kingdom. If someone has, say, a musical talent there is nothing at all wrong with developing that in order to serve God with it. There is nothing unspiritual about using and developing natural talents in the Kingdom of God, and this is true with children just as much as with adults. But talents are not ministries.

Ministries also need to be distinguished from the gifts of the Holy Spirit. The gifts are the tools we need to do a particular job. It is not right to say that people have a prophetic ministry just because they prophesy. We should all be prophesying but it does not mean that we will all have a prophetic ministry. Similarly although I have led a number of evangelistic meetings it does not mean I am an evangelist. The gifts of the Spirit are vitally important, but they are not of themselves ministries.

A ministry is something we can only receive when we have come to Jesus. After all, a non-Christian can be talented. But ministry is a Jesus-given ability to serve God in a particular way. The categories of ministries are never closed. Someone might have, for example, a dance ministry, a music ministry, drama ministry, preaching ministry, evangelistic ministry, prophetic ministry, practical ministry and so on. One friend of mine has a very interesting flag-waving ministry!

When dealing with ministries and especially when seeing our children's own ministries develop it is important that we know what we are talking about.

What is a ministry?

The greatest example we have is, of course, Jesus. He did not arrive in impressive style and full of self-importance to build a vast platform for his own operations. He came as a servant to give his life away and finally to die for the sake of those in every generation whom he came to serve. The very word "minister" actually means "servant" which tells us immediately that anyone aspiring to a ministry is aspiring to servanthood. When we look at some of the mega-ministries there are around we can sometimes be left wondering where the servant element is. Expecting to stay in five-star hotels, wait in the VIP lounge at airports and be driven by chauffeur is all very nice from time to time as a bonus, but when we come to expect it as a right and as a part of our own very significant international mega-ministry it becomes very questionable. One day we will have to answer to someone who was born in a stable and who had nowhere to lay his head.

Most ministries are not glamorous. A few are but most are not. Even those that look glamorous, like beach missions in Miami, often turn out to involve pressure and heartache from time to time behind the scenes! Our children must not run away with the idea that their newly-discovered ministry will automatically involve aeroplanes, tours of America and magazine coverage. Some may, but most will not. The important thing is not how visible and high-profile is my ministry, it is a matter of knowing what God has called me to and getting on with the job whatever it may be. Probably ninety-nine per cent of all ministry takes place by people no one has ever heard of.

The truth is that we all have a ministry. Often, however, we are looking for something grand, something with status and recognition. When it does not quite work out the way we want, we get disappointed. The essence of ministry is that it is not what we want but what God wants that is important. Children have potential ministries just as much as adults. Once discovered and nurtured, they can blossom and flourish even in childhood if we will give them room in our churches to develop.

Many ministries operate in practical areas. Just because a person is not a preacher, teacher, evangelist, apostle or pastor does not mean that he or she does not have a valid ministry. If we really believe that a ministry can be anything that we are called to which has at its core the object of serving God, we realise that the possibilities are endless. Many people have very practical ministries. Administration, serving meals, packing food parcels and many, many other things are all ways of ministering to or serving God.

Can my ministry be nice?

Some people have built a theology which says that what I enjoy doing must be wrong and what God wants me to do must be hard! I once told someone I was so glad God had not called me to be a missionary abroad. Almost at once I was told I must not say that because God might make me do it just to show me!

Sometimes people point to verses like Isaiah 55:8–9: ''For my thoughts are not your thoughts nor are your ways my ways, declares the Lord. As the heavens are higher than the earth, so are my ways higher than your ways and my thoughts than your thoughts.'' The conclusion they draw is that God always wants to purge us or break our wills and that to prove to him that we are willing to go his way rather than ours we must be prepared to do something really hard and unpleasant!

There are, of course, times when we may have to take a step of obedience when we would prefer not to. When Lynda and I moved away to the West Country in 1984 I really did not want to go. As far as we were concerned at the time, it was for ever. But God gave us a specific word that said we should go. I got the job I applied for even though, to be honest, I made no special effort at the interview. Although we received unclear advice from our Fellowship with different leaders saying different things, we knew that God had said "Go". Six years later when we moved back home to Littlehampton we were very much further on spiritually as a result of all we experienced whilst we were away.

As a general rule, however, we need to understand that God and Us are actually on the same side! So often the impression is given that it is like a battle: God-v-Me. But God is my Father, I am his son. He has my best interests at heart. His desire is to release me into my ministry, not make it hard like an obstacle course followed by an endurance test!

We need to understand that verses like Isaiah 55:8–9 were spoken to a rebellious nation which had turned its back on God. The position with people who love God and are going on with him is altogether different. For us the true perspective is not so much Isaiah 55:8–9, but Psalm 37:4: "Delight yourself in the Lord and he will give you the desires of your heart." The reason for this is that God is the one who gave us our desires in the first place!

When I was at university the one thing I used to dream of was going full-time on the road in a travelling ministry. That is what I always wanted to do more than anything else in the world. The idea of travelling round to different churches and fellowships, having my roots firmly placed in one, was what I really wanted to do. But I had run away with the idea that all this was simply my own desires. God probably wanted me to be a missionary abroad for no other reason than that I was not keen to go!

Someone then said something to me which in time changed my entire perspective. It was that the things you like doing are the very things that God has probably called you to do. To start with I thought this was theologically unsound. After all, ministries are not meant to be nice and enjoyable – are they? Gradually the truth sank in. Now, miraculously, ten years later, here I am doing just that. God is good!

What a contrast in attitudes there is between Isaiah 55:8–9, on the one hand, and Psalm 37:4 on the other. The one positively oozes condemnation and heaviness, the other, release and lightness. God has called us to the latter! We need to paint a true picture when it comes to encouraging our own children into ministry. What a tragedy it would be if children in the Kingdom were looking over their shoulders for persecution, heaviness and obedience involving spiritual nasties, rather than believing for a release in what they are good at and enjoy doing.

Discovering children's ministries
Reference has already been made to children and young people in the Bible who had ministries and who were busy getting on with the job. So, for example, Samuel was ministering to the Lord as a priest even as a child. We have suggested that if Samuel were to appear in most of our churches today he would be shunted off into a separate room to make a model of Noah's ark using the inside of an old toilet roll and a yoghurt pot! It is highly unlikely that we would let him minister to the Lord in our meetings.

We need to understand that with children who are Christians, God is already shaping their lives and creating ministries. Just as the Spirit of the Lord moved on Samson as a child (Judges 13:25), we need to expect the same to happen with our own children – especially as we are under the new covenant in an age of the Holy Spirit!

I preached for the first time at the age of sixteen. Although it was pretty rough and ready I can remember the fellowship leaders encouraging me and letting me have another go. After a few times they told me they thought I had a preaching ministry which needed to be developed. I always enjoyed preaching and began to feel that as I was speaking God was actually working in people's lives. The thing that spurred me on more than anything else was the encouragement of my church leaders. What they were in effect doing was confirming me as a person, recognising a ministry and giving me the room to grow in it. I am still grateful to them because I know that leaders can either encourage ministry or squash it flat.

I have prayed specifically with numerous children to help them discover their ministry. It is quite useful that I was called into Christian ministry at the age of nine. Now I can pray intelligently with nine-year-olds. On the other hand I had the frustration of having to wait twenty years before launching out, so hopefully I can also pray intelligently with ninety-year-olds!

Often I have found children who know that God has called them to something but do not have a clue what it is. This is excellent! I shows that the Holy Spirit had already started to work on their lives. All we need to do is provide encouragement and pray with them on an ongoing basis so that when the time is right they will know which direction to go. After all, God is more keen for us to do his will than we are to do it! He is not going to leave us totally in the dark about his plans for our lives and in the lives of the children we serve. But we must not expect to know any more than the next step.

We all want to see a map of our lives in advance so that we know where we are going next! It hardly ever works out that way. We are called to live by faith and not by sight.

136

Even the children of Israel had to learn this. They were on the banks of a river. The Promised Land was just in front of them on the other side. The were all exited – after all, this was the fulfilment of a long-standing promise they had had to wait patiently for. But where do you start when a whole land is in front of you? God showed the leader, Joshua, something significant. Although there was much ground to claim all they had to do was go to Jericho. All they were called to do was take the first step.

There is an old Chinese proverb that says "The longest journey starts with the first step". If we could get that into our lives we would go a long way towards quelling our frustrations and those of our children when it all seems to be taking rather longer to fulfil than we had anticipated.

Some children actually know what God has called them to do. After a recent meeting where I was encouraging children to ask God what he wanted for their lives I was amazed at some of their responses. One young girl told me that God had called her to be a nurse. A young lad said he felt God wanted him to be an evangelist. Someone else said he knew God wanted him to work abroad.

It is also encouraging to find that response from children actually jolts adults into action. Often if I have a team working with me I find that team members have to get down to some serious business with God just to keep up with the children! On one occasion one of the youngest members of the team felt a calling to go abroad and serve God in linguistic skills. She is now developing her Spanish and is planning to work in South America.

At a recent weekend away for children I was encouraging the children in prophecy. As this was taking place around me I began to realise that it was important for me to be involved too and not be the slick professional at the front with everything all sewn up! I began to prophesy over some children and then began to pray for one girl in particular who was ten years old. I began to prophesy over her too.

137

It was not all that easy because her parents were in the room as they were actually the leaders for the weekend! I could hardly believe the words that were coming out of my mouth. I stepped out in faith and trusted it was right! According to this word God was preparing her for a ministry that would take her around the world. She would speak to the nations. While I was speaking she was crying her heart out. Immediately after the session I spoke to her parents who told me in a very casual and laid-back manner that it was not the first time a word like this had been brought to her. My first reaction was relief – but this was swiftly followed by praising God that he should have confirmed such an exciting call to such a young girl.

Even though most of our children will not end up with a jet-setting international ministry, it is important that they begin to ask God what his plans for their lives are. There is nothing more fulfilling than being in the centre of God's will.

Full-time ministry?
There is a popular myth around that when you get into full-time ministry you have made it! It almost suggests that full-time ministry is a reward for the spiritual, for the special. Of course, all this is nonsense.

Virtually everyone I have known who has been keen to follow the Lord has felt it will all end up in full-time ministry. Many good friends have started to grow old gracefully, marking time until they can suddenly throw in their job and go full-time! The truth is that not everyone is called to it. Even those who are soon to realise that instead of suddenly having made it, they have started at the bottom.

When I started off in full-time ministry in October 1988 I realised that, having left my professional job where I had been in a senior position, I was now at the bottom of the pile. I felt like an eleven-year-old who has just left the top of the juniors as a big boy only to find himself on the first day in senior school where he cannot even find his way round the corridors. In my local church I had been able to contribute at leadership level. Now I was a totally unknown new boy with a national ministry. I started off doing bookings which landed me in little children's groups, taking traditional Sunday school anniversary services and little hole-in-the-corner fringe meetings!

In the early days especially I used to get a number of Ishmael's reject bookings. I am very grateful to him for his friendship, now more than ever, and he was a great help in getting me started. But, arriving at some churches, I knew immediately why I was there and not Ishmael, even before I went in! Often I felt I could almost hear him laughing! "Lord," I would cry, "you have called me to be a prophetic voice to the nation, a national leader, to shape the Church – so what am I doing at this little children's meeting sampling a piece of Auntie Mavis' birthday cake?"

What has all this to do with ministries? Simply that we often think full-time ministry is glamorous. The reality is that it can be equally as frustrating as life was before giving up our jobs. Our children need to understand that full-time ministry is not the be all and end all. If we were all in full-time ministry, how could we be salt and light in the world? We need Christian dentists, shop-keepers, factory workers, accountants, nurses and so on. Our children must know that it is not unspiritual to have a job. Some of the most spiritual people I have ever known have had ordinary jobs. Similarly some of the most non-impressive lifestyles are led by people in full-time ministry. We must stop the rot in our thinking and recognise that the idea of full-time ministry as a reward for the spiritual is simply not true.

It sounds trite and almost patronising to say it, but it is true that we are all in full-time ministry right where we are. It is so important that Christian are active in every area of life so that we can show Jesus in word and deed to a non-Christian society.

It is easy to fall into the trap of thinking that all call to ministry must refer to adult ministry. We tend to think that although children can be *called* while they are young they cannot actually do anything until they are old. Sometimes, of course, this is true. For example, a child with a calling to be a doctor in Brazil obviously cannot go and do it straight away. But that is not to say that there is no ministry rôle for that child in the meantime. Similarly, many children will be called to a ministry that will be much more low key. There is nothing to stop those ministries beginning in childhood. Some of the more "conventional" ministries can also start to be exercised in childhood. Those called to be an evangelist, for example, can begin right where they are, at school and among their friends in the neighbourhood.

Although it is important to recognise and encourage ministry, it is also important that we do not put labels on children too soon. Ministries develop. It would be a tragedy if we put children's ministries in a box at an early age and restricted further potential development. For example, as a teenager I thought my ministry was in evangelism. Later I realised that although God has used me in this way it is not my main ministry. It took me a little while to realise that my calling is actually to the Church and that the main thrust is to help shape its development in our generation. Fortunately I was given the freedom to develop in this area and to put on one side areas of ministry that others are much better equipped to deal with.

Practical ministries

It is important that we recognise practical ministries as valid and do not put them down in our thinking. It is important for everyone to have a real part to play, and if someone's role in the church is practical then it is just as much a ministry as anything else.

There is however an important point that needs to be made here and which never seems to be said. It will have a direct bearing on what we teach our children about ministries.

Sometimes I believe we have sold individuals short by confining them to practical jobs. Often these people are capable of giving a lot more than this, but never move on either because they are not given the chance or because they have a poor view of themselves and consider themselves inadequate.

Take for example the job of putting out the chairs or setting up the PA system for the Sunday morning meeting. Naturally it is important that someone is responsible for these tasks. If it is not done, no one will have a seat and no one will be able to hear anything! But often it is all left to the person with the practical ministry. They soon get labelled as the practical person and soon no one believes that they can do anything else.

The Church should be constantly training up new people and developing ministries. Frankly, the chairs *could* be put out by a non-Christian. Although it is someone's "ministry", it is a mistake to think that this person cannot ever move on to a slightly higher calling. On the other hand, there are some who like the comfort of being stuck in the rut of the practical who need to be encouraged to take steps of faith and develop into other areas.

It is often easier to concentrate more on the chairs, overhead projector, sound and lighting – the mechanical side – than on what God actually wants to say and do. Whilst thanking God for practical ministries, let us not be satisfied with dumping the messy practical jobs on someone and dressing it all up in spiritual clothes by referring to it as their ministry which they are then stuck with for ever and a day! It is particularly important, if we have tried to encourage young people to be involved by giving them practical responsibilities in the church, that we do not fall into the trap of thinking that is all they are ever going to be good for.

Training children

If our children are beginning to exercise ministries now, we have to give thought to training them. I have found that the most effective form of training is what is caught rather than what is taught, that is, in-life discipleship. Personal example is not just the best form of discipleship, it is the only form of discipleship.

The key to training lies not in a residential college with a diploma at the end – after all, children normally have schools to go to! The key lies in effective leadership example. This is such an important topic it will be looked at in more detail in Chapter 14. For now we need simply to keep in mind that it is our example and input which will make the difference between children praying about the direction of their own ministries or simply doing some colouring until the adult meeting is over.

Take, for example, praise and worship. One of my pet hates is to find leaders at family celebration events who choose to opt out. When I am encouraging everyone to unwind, relax and get stuck in to the praise and worship, there is nothing more galling than to find the *leaders* hunting round for a chair to sit on. I would not mind if they were hunting for a chair to dance on or to jump off, but to sit down and opt out, as well as being bad manners, is actually suggesting fundamental disapproval. We will never see our children free in praise and worship if we are not prepared to be free in it ourselves.

As part of training it is important to stretch the children in terms of their own experience. I am amazed as I travel around the country to find that even today in many of our churches there are adults who still cannot pray out loud. Very occasionally this is a personality issue, and a real introvert will by nature find it hard. More often however it is a cultural issue with no demands being made on anyone other than the one-man minister! If we find it hard to pray out loud we will find it even harder to pray for (say) the person sitting next to us. It will then be almost impossible to prophesy over them!

A good way to stop this attitude and culture being perpetuated within the Church is to begin with the children. We need to get them praying together. We need also to get them praying for each other. We then need to move on to see them prophesying over each other. And if we as leaders are having difficulties ourselves it goes without saying that we need to get ourselves sorted out first!

Often there is a stilted feeling of embarrassment when we first try this. Everyone feels awkward. But we need to take the trouble to press through the pain barrier to see the children free to pray. I have started doing this recently at Praise Parties where I sometimes ask everyone to get into groups of two and pray for each other. After a couple of minutes they swap over. I insist that there is no chatting, just praying. It is amazing how quickly children – and adults – get used to it! Very soon they are there, arms round the shoulder, praying effectively for each other.

It is important to take time to develop this. Even in a church environment where this kind of approach would be the norm, it is important to keep exercising the muscle of praying together.

Ministries and character

Once our children are beginning to step out in their ministries or are praying seriously about it, there is an important aspect we need to teach them.

Gifting, however brilliant and however anointed, is not enough. Character must match the gifting. Sometimes the reason we have to wait so long for the fulfilment of God's plans for our future ministry is simply that we need time for our characters and lifestyle to catch up with our gifting.

There is nothing worse than a person who is gifted but whose lifestyle and character fall badly short. A good biblical example of this is Jonah.

143

Jonah would never have been chosen to go to Nineveh if he had not been gifted. He was clearly a gifted man. But his character was completely unstable. The biblical account starts with rebellion to God because Jonah considered it unfair and unjust that God might forgive such a wicked nation as the Assyrians when they repented. Once he had been rescued by the fish and given a second chance, his character was still no better. He sat outside the city of Nineveh where he had been privileged to see a whole nation repent. There, feeling miserable and depressed, he hoped that perhaps God would change his mind and punish them after all. He accepted the fact the *he* had been rescued when he had done wrong, but could not accept that God wanted to rescue this nation that had done wrong. He then accepted the fact that God caused a plant to grow quickly to shade him from the sun, but could not accept that God could allow a worm to nibble at the roots to demolish it!

I would love to be able to read that the story had a happy ending but the Bible does not say that it did. The Bible tells it as it is and shows us that Jonah's character was completely out of line with his gifting.

Preparing young people for leadership

A serious problem that faces many churches is that we have set our requirements for new leaders so high that no one is able to comply with them. Many leaders expect potential leaders to be as we are now, rather than as we ourselves were when we first came into leadership!

Most of us were fairly ignorant when we first started off in leadership. As time went on we learned and developed. Although the basic gifting was always there we were inexperienced with dealing with people, impatient, insensitive and so on. Now when we are looking round for new leadership in the church we tut, shrug our shoulders and claim that we have no one coming along. What we mean is, no one as good as we think we are!

If we really take the role of children seriously in the church, if we are seeing them moving in the gifts of the Spirit as children and discovering their own ministries, then I would expect them to be coming into team leadership at a relatively early age.

Leaders must have maturity as well as gifting. People in their early twenties are normally thought of as lacking in experience. Yet I believe we are seeing some very experienced younger people around in the church nowadays. Just recently whilst confirming arrangements to visit a church I was told of a young people's team who had led meetings there just a few weeks before. These people had seen healings, deliverance, prophecy and so on—and all the team were teenagers! Certainly young leaders tend to be the visionaries and are able to see through the dross to the realities behind situations. I believe the time has come to release some of these younger people into corporate leadership.

In a team situation which is balanced with older leaders, younger people can make a tremendous contribution. The fastest growing church here on the south coast has a young forward-looking leadership team. Of course we need maturity, but youth and maturity are not such opposites as many people think. Naturally we need older men and women. The problem has been that for too long leadership has been exclusively for older people. My prayer is that we will see a release of anointed younger leaders.

Young leadership is not a new concept. In the first chapter of the book of Numbers, Moses organised his people by taking a census of all who could go to war, all who would be able to lead Israel into victory. His instruction was to include everyone from twenty years old and above provided they were able to go to war. Although he was prepared to take young warriors, no one was suggesting that non-warriors should be included!

Sometimes it happened in the Old Testament that the

older was called to serve the younger. Examples of this include Esau who had to serve Jacob, the sons of Jacob (i.e. Israel) who had to serve Joseph, Manasseh who had to serve Ephraim, and so on. When that promising young lad Elihu heard the inadequate advice Job's three "comforters" had given, he knew he had a word from the Lord. He said:

> "I am young in years, and you are old; that is why I was fearful, not daring to tell you what I know. I thought 'Age should speak; advanced years should teach wisdom.' But it is the spirit in a man, the breath of the Almighty, that gives him understanding. It is not only who are wise, not only the aged who understand what is right." (Job 32:6–9)

No one would want in any way to sidestep the teaching of the New Testament and the emphasis of stability and maturity that underlies every requirement relating to potential leaders we read about in the letters. But this must be tempered with the raw edge of youth as well. After all, the disciples were hardly models of wisdom and maturity! Peter denied Jesus three times that we know of, yet Jesus said of him "On this rock I will build my church, and the gates of Hades will not overcome it" (Matthew 16:17–18).

Unlearned fishermen who had never been to Bible college and who, spiritually, did not know the difference between a binnacle and a barnacle suddenly found themselves at the forefront of this new thing called the Kingdom of God!

A ministry of success?

Whilst it is very important to encourage children to discover and develop their ministries, there is one very important factor to bear in mind.

Ministry does not always have to do with achievement. Sometimes when people talk about ministries they become very success-orientated. Whilst there is nothing at all wrong with God-centred success (see for example the lives of Abraham, Joseph, David and Solomon), we must be careful not to give the impression especially to children that to please God we must achieve success for him.

Sometimes it is not so much what we achieve but the way we go about what we are doing that is important. Sometimes we may "achieve" little and yet still have done all that God requires of us. Who we are counts far more that what we achieve. As someone has neatly put it, "I am a human being not a human doing"! Many of us have been taught that we have been "saved to serve". I do not believe this is quite true. We have been saved to love God for its own sake. It is then out of love for him that we are called to serve.

There is a part of most of us that likes to try to measure success. An evangelist likes to chalk up converts, we like to feel that sick people we pray for are healed and so on. Yet I have found that success often cannot be measured. I have quite often led all-age celebration meetings which have gone really well with a tremendous sense of God's presence yet with virtually no response to ministry.

Sometimes it is the other way round. I remember once leading a children's day at a national conference for a well-known Christian organisation. All the adults (about 1,000) were in the plush conference hall. All the children (about 50) were with us in a remote upstairs room. It was obvious that the children did not want to be there but had no choice because Mum and Dad were at the conference. The day was really hard work with a very lukewarm response. When we did some teaching on power and being filled with the Holy Spirit, quite a number responded and began worshipping in tongues. The problem was that the general feeling of the meeting was awful! The atmosphere was heavy and miserable with most of the children apathetic and lethargic. We may have been able to chalk up a few "successes" but so what? The meeting was not good as far as I was concerned. In fact I had to cheer myself up with a Chinese takeaway afterwards during which I lost my car keys, 200 miles from home! But that is another story.

Taking Children Seriously

The key to all this is not necessarily success, but fulfilment. Children need to know what God wants for their lives, not what appears to them to be glamorous and attractive.

Chapter 11

Building Faith

There is sometimes more fear than faith in the Kingdom of God. And our attitudes as adults rub off on our children.

When I gave up my job as a solicitor and head of the legal department of a local authority, I was amazed at the support and encouragement given to me by my non-Christian boss. He said that he admired my stand and was amazed that someone's faith could lead him to actually give up his job! I was grateful for his support.

When I told people in the Kingdom what I believed God had called me to do it met with instant caution. Mutterings about my financial responsibilities, my wife and small child, what if it all goes wrong and so on. I was kept going by the support of those who knew me and my certainty that God had called me and in the end that was all that mattered. Rather like Abraham who had to leave everything behind in obedience even though he did not know where he was going, I knew I had to take this step of faith.

Those of us who were brought up within the Church have had our thinking shaped by what we have seen around us. When it comes to faith and believing supernaturally that God will do things, we have often seen nothing said and, more to the point, have seen nothing happen. We have grown up knowing that the Bible teaches faith, knowing that God *can* do great wonders but seeing very little out of the ordinary actually happening in our own lives.

If our children are going to become great faith warriors in their own right, they need to look to us for example and leadership. If we are not there ourselves we will never be able to take our children there.

As with all great spiritual concepts, faith is something which can be made simple enough for a child to understand. The problem is that there has been a lot of woolly thinking on faith and we are often not too sure what we believe ourselves on the subject!

Yet I firmly believe that children can understand faith and can develop their own faith level while they are still children. I remember some little girls who were once moaning on a Sunday afternoon about wanting some sweets. Dad told them that if they really wanted sweets they should pray about it just as they would about other things. So they all sat down and prayed on the spot. After only a few minutes there was a knock at the front door. An unexpected guest arrived complete with sweets for the children! This might sound like a sickly little story (I'm not sure it would happen quite like this in our house!) but it shows that even at the most basic level children can begin to understand what faith is all about.

We need to start with the basics so that we can get to grips with the issues for ourselves and then we need to bring the whole thing within easy reach of our children.

What faith is not
We are talking here not about the faith involved in becoming a Christian but rather about living in faith and seeing the supernatural happen in our own lives and in the lives of our children.

To see what faith is, let's first remind ourselves what it is not!

1. It is not a commodity to be purchased
Some Christians assume they are not spiritual enough to have faith. We may feel that if only we could pray more and read out Bibles more than maybe one day we would work ourselves up to be able to cope with this great thing called faith! The truth is that although spirituality is an

essential part of going on with God, it is not the price to be paid for faith. None of us are as "spiritual" as we would like, but if God had to wait until we had earned the right to exercise faith by being spiritual enough, none of us would ever be ready. Thank God for grace!

2. *It is not something we can work up*
I have often heard the expression, "If only I had more faith . . ." The implication is that faith can somehow be mustered up. We may feel that if everything were really good in our lives we should be able to grab a lump of faith – we should be able to work it up. But the fact that we may not be exercising much faith does not mean there is something major wrong with us. Thankfully faith is not something that it is possible to work up. This is because faith is a gift to us, a response to a specific word from God into our lives.

3. *It is not about getting what we want*
Faith exists so that we can give God what *he* wants. Faith teaching can sometimes give the impression that as God's children we are like spoilt brats who can demand what *we* want and get it. Those who teach a divine *right* to health, wealth and happiness usually start off with the premise that faith is there to enable me to get what I want, not to enable me to deliver what God wants. They suggest that faith operates mainly in the realm of financial prosperity. The reality is that life is not always like that. I am here for God's sake – God is not here for my sake!

I have been privileged to make several visits to Eastern Europe to lead meetings. To say to my brothers and sisters there that they are poor because they do not have enough faith would be pathetic and insulting. The fact is that we do not always get what we want when we want. Jesus was not into financial prosperity as far as we know. He was born in poverty and ascended without leaving a vast financial empire to fund the Kingdom. However, God did supply a coin in the mouth of the fish to pay the temple tax and Jesus did have all his needs met.

Whilst we should not go to the other extreme (which I have also come across) of thinking that there is something good – something "spiritual" – in poverty, we do need to have our thinking clear. It is worth remembering that when Peter, the apostle, was in prison he was prayed for and released. When Paul, the apostle, was in prison he was prayed for and was not released. In fact he was killed. When Peter preached three thousand people were swept into the Kingdom. When Stephen preached he was stoned to death.

Getting our perspective right is important. If our children see that our teaching and our words do not marry up with our experience, they will become disillusioned. Instead of beginning their own adventures of faith, they may be put off completely. They will assume that they are part of a Kingdom of words not of power. Not only may they become disappointed, but they may also think as they get older that if we do not have it right on faith (a basic teaching element in the Kingdom of God) how can they be sure we have got it right in other areas as well?

What faith is!
Faith operates as a response to God after he has taken the initiative in speaking a specific word into our lives.

Our actions to step out in faith must always be preceded by a word from God. That is why Romans 10:17 tells us that faith comes by hearing and hearing by the word of God. This is a clear biblical principle. For example, Abraham was able to take the risk of leaving his familiar surroundings and everything else behind and setting off for Destination Unknown only because God had spoken to him and told him to go. Abraham's faith was a response to God speaking a word into his life (see Genesis 12). Similarly Peter was able to step out of the boat and walk on the water because Jesus had said to him "Come" (Matthew 14:29). We can afford to take risks, live dangerously and step on to thin ice only if God has said so.

When we are teaching a subject like faith to children it is vital that all these concepts are illustrated from our personal experience rather than from an entirely theoretical perspective. Being a children's worker today is much more than flannelgraphs and birthday cake. It is about living in the Spirit ourselves so that we can build into the children's lives issues like faith, having actually been there ourselves.

My own experience of faith and therefore acting on a word from God has involved me in really practical steps including the following specific examples: selling my car, moving 200 miles away, not accepting an offer of going abroad to preach, leaving my job and abandoning my career, seeing specific individuals healed, praying money in, initiating tours, and so on. I am not always very good at listening but I am prepared to act on what I believe God has said to me. I have found that when I explain it to children in concrete terms like this you can hear a pin drop! They want to know about faith. They want to make it their experience. But they will never learn in a radical in-life way if we simply regurgitate the printed Bible notes and then ask the children to do a drawing!

When we teach familiar Bible stories like Abraham in the context of faith, we need to explain how relevant they are to the real issues of life. The Bible must come alive in a real dynamic way! For example, when we teach our children that God was speaking to Abraham we can go on to explain how God wants to say things to us. Obviously we need to share our own personal experiences with them to put flesh on the bones. Then we need to explain how Abraham acted even though it seemed a foolish and dangerous thing to do. Here we can give examples of when this has actually happened in our own lives. Finally we need to teach how

God fulfilled his word by bringing Abraham into the land, drawing the parallel with how God wants to fulfil his word in our lives. At the same time we need to teach the Bible as it is. We see, for example, that Abraham in the very next section (Genesis 12:10–20) decides to go to Egypt without a word from God. He acts out of human expediency and fear rather than faith, and ends up telling everyone that his wife is his sister for fear of losing her.

We need to base all that we teach firmly on the Bible, fleshed out with our own experience. There is no shortage of material in the Bible but it is possible to misrepresent it. It is sad to see the way many great Bible stories are reduced to trite little tales for the children. We need to rediscover them in terms of allowing God to speak through them afresh at all levels in the church.

How does God speak?
If faith comes as a response to a word from God, it is important to teach our children the different ways in which God speaks to us. It is only when they are learning to hear from God themselves that they will be able to take steps of faith.

1. From the Bible
At one time what was often taught in effect was that God's sole means of communication was through giving us a verse from the Bible. This is, of course, a very good example of how God speaks to us. But we are not talking here about finding some general verses we feel may apply to us. Instead we are talking about receiving a specific word into our situation. In a way this is a form of prophetic communication because God is taking a verse and using it out of context to apply in the specifics of the individual situation. For example, when we moved to the West Country (where we stayed for six years) God gave us a word from John 15: ''For you have not chosen me but I have chosen you and ordained

154

you that you should GO and bring forth fruit" (NKJV). Both Lynda and I knew that God was speaking to us to clinch what had been a very difficult decision with lots of uncertainty until that point.

There are three major dangers connected with receiving Bible verses subjectively to guide us in our own individual situations.

The first problem is that we can easily scratch around and find a verse to say exactly what we want. We can all find a verse which helps us out or which says what we think someone else needs to hear! That is not what it is about at all. The verses must always be received in circumstances where they are a specific word from God to us.

The second danger is that we can (as I have heard it put) "plead the promises" blindly – and run into trouble. I once heard about someone who tried to walk on water. He reasoned that Peter did it and as it was in the Bible it must be possible for him to do it. He drowned. We need to claim in faith only what God says to us specifically. Peter stood not so much on the water but on Jesus' word to him, "Come!" I have also experienced this problem with healing where we "claim" general promises but are then left scratching our heads wondering why someone has not been healed!

The third danger is religion. I have met people who need a scripture before they will do anything. Whilst it is quite true to say that the Bible is the prime source of guidance, we do have to be a little careful. Some people cannot accept any other way of God speaking. It has to be a Bible verse, they say, or it is not God. This leads to contraptions like Promise Boxes where you put in your tweezers and hook out a scripture. If you happen to pick out something like "Judas went out and hanged himself" it does not count and you get another go!

2. Gifts of the Spirit
As soon as we see our children beginning to gain experience

in prophecy we can expect that God will begin to give them words and pictures for one another. We can also expect specific words of knowledge. These can be a great encouragement, especially when someone who hardly knows you gives you a word that confirms something that God had already been showing you. For example, since I started on the road full-time in October 1988, I have received four prophecies that my work would go international. At first I thought God was only joking! Now I find it is starting to be a reality. In the last twelve months I have been to Poland twice, and to Yugoslavia. I also have invitation to India and Canada. I can still hardly believe it! There is no reason why our children cannot be used in similar ways.

With prophecy there is always room for error. Speaking personally I would not base a major decision on a single prophecy. However, a single prophecy might combine with a number of other things to confirm God's word to me.

3. *Resources*
Books, tapes and videos can bring great ministry into our homes which God may use specifically to speak to us. Sometimes what is said or read may speak straight into our lives. Often something that is alluded to or referred to in passing will be the right word. It has happened that whilst I have been preaching God has spoken to me about issues wholly unrelated to the subject of the talk!

4. *Circumstances*
Circumstances are a more dubious way of hearing God. Although God can and often does speak to us through our circumstances, there is an in-built difficulty. Sometimes our circumstances are not right. If therefore we are relying only on this we can become confused. Sometimes we need to take authority over the circumstances rather than allow the circumstances to take authority over us! I was once involved in praying for someone who was dying but because God

actually spoke to us about restoring and healing we claimed and believed that word rather than the circumstances which the doctors said would result in death. In that particular case the lady was quite miraculously healed.

To the extent that circumstances do guide us, they will normally be used to *confirm* something that is already stirring in us, rather than being the prime source of guidance.

5. *Others*

The other possibilities are endless! God will use anything that we can understand to speak to us.

I have sometimes been chatting informally to someone when quite suddenly something was said in conversation which I knew was God speaking to me! It was not put into prophetic words – it was simply a very informal chat!

One person in our fellowship was driving in her car before she was a Christian and came to some roadworks where she saw a sign saying "One way". She had heard about Jesus but this signpost was the clincher and she became a Christian!

A friend of ours was once watching the film "Jesus of Nazareth" on TV. When it got to the baptism scene she knew that God was showing her that she should be baptised. Although she had been a Christian for some time, she was a little ambivalent about baptism, not having been convinced that baptism was necessary. It was whilst watching the TV that God showed her that she should be baptised.

When looking at the different ways God speaks to us there is an important point to bear in mind. God will never speak to us in a way which will contradict or go against Scripture. Everything must always be weighed with Scripture. Generally too, God will speak to us in a number of different ways at around the same time so as to confirm what he is saying.

Encouraging children to hear the voice of God
In my experience children have an enormous capacity not only to perceive spiritual truth but to understand what God wants to say to them. Naturally they have to be taught properly. Even our terminology can be confusing to them. Phrases like "hearing God's voice", for example, can imply that God will speak in an audible voice which of course happens only very rarely.

A lady in our fellowship had been praying for years for her husband to become a Christian. Then one day God spoke to her and showed her this would actually happen. She mentioned it to her two children who both told her that they already knew their Dad would become a Christian. Somehow whilst the children had been praying they knew on the inside that it would happen. Eight years later it did!

I have already mentioned the fact that I was called to serve the Lord at the age of nine. Although I only had a child's perception at that stage I still knew deep down inside that God had "spoken" to me and called me. Twenty years later I handed in my notice!

I have prayed for many children on my travels who know God has called them to something even if they don't know exactly what. I have seen children literally in tears as God has challenged them and spoken right into their lives.

It is normally adults who have problems with the idea that children can understand what God wants to say. Some of us – including children's leaders, not to say church leaders – are struggling in these areas ourselves! Once we get a vision of what is possible with our children and as soon as we are prepared to be challenged ourselves in these areas, we see our children learning what taking steps of faith is all about.

Faith without a word?
From all that has been said about faith it is clear that steps of faith must be preceded by a word from the Lord. The

question then is whether faith can operate when there is no preceding word. The answer to that appears to be No, but there is one exception – where God gives a special gift of faith.

One of the specific gifts of the Holy Spirit is faith. It is one of the nine gifts listed in 1 Corinthians 12:8–10. It is a gift which God gives in a particular situation that tells us we can believe God for the issue involved. It is initiated by God and as with all of the gifts it is available to all Christians. Faith is one of the tools we are issued with in our spiritual gift toolkit which is given to us as soon as we are filled with the Spirit.

In the same way that we may receive a prophecy, word of knowledge or one of the other gifts, a gift of faith may well be available to help us deal with a given situation.

Once children have made a start with words of knowledge and prophecy, gifts of faith will follow naturally. Once again it is the job of the leader to lead in this area. The whole issue of faith is something that can be communicated to children in a way that they will understand. As with all these things it is easier to talk about it than do it and it is so very important that we do not opt for the comfort of talking only and not doing.

Hanging on
I once saw a poster which said "Faith isn't faith until it's all you're hanging on to"! Once we know what God has said we need to wait patiently until that word is fulfilled. Sometimes this involves heartache and frustration as God's idea of timing and ours do not always happily coincide. It came as quite a shock to me on one occasion to realise that God is building his Kingdom and is in no real hurry – after all it will last through all eternity! I on the other hand was hardly able to contain myself waiting for things to be fulfilled in my own life!

It often happens that like Joseph we receive a word and

then immediately realise that the situation we are in is completely opposite to the word. We are then faced with the choice of either believing God's word, even though we cannot see any realistic prospect of it all coming to pass, or of simply believing the circumstances and forgetting the word. It is easy then to fall into the middle ground. We don't reject the word but on the other hand we cannot see that anything is going to change our circumstances, so we find ourselves in a kind of prophetic stalemate!

As someone once prayed, "Lord, I want more patience – and I want it now!" Patience is what it is all about. Both for us and for our children who are beginning to take steps of faith, we need to be able to hang on in there even when it all seems to be taking a long time. As an action-man, raring to go, the need to deal with frustration has been one of the hardest things for me to have to cope with!

One of the great discoveries I have made in hanging on in faith is that if God has said something we can be sure that it is already done in heaven. We may not see it yet from where we stand but as far as God is concerned it is already done. That is why we can call things that are not as though they are – because God has promised to deliver! It is rather like my writing a letter to you and then posting it. As far as I am concerned it is all done – I have written it and posted it. But as far as you are concerned you have not received it. Now if I phone you and tell you that the letter is in the post you will know that even though you have not received it yet, you will!

Faith in a vacuum?
When we look at issues such as faith it is easy to end up looking at them in a vacuum. We can dot our doctrinal i's and cross our doctrinal t's but at the end of the day, having a systematic theology about faith that we can teach our children is not enough.

Faith does not operate in a vacuum. It operates in the

realities of our day-to-day lives. Faith has to do with issues like healing, seeing people becoming Christians, seeing our financial needs met, using the gifts of the Spirit, releasing ministries as well as in specific personal issues.

We cannot teach our children "faith" one week then go on and do something else with them next week. If we do it is likely that we are retreating into the safety of talking doctrine rather than pioneering in active in-life participation! We must stay with it to ensure that principles of faith are worked into their lives. A church that is all talk and no action is worse than a church that is not even all talk! Passive acquiescence about seeing faith released in children is worse than not even understanding what faith is all about.

God is looking for action, not just words. This is particularly true in the whole important area of seeing real faith being developed in the lives of children. Let us rise to the challenge first in our own lives and then pass on the lessons to our children. Who knows – we may end up learning an awful lot about faith from them!

Chapter 12

Praise and Worship

One of the most significant changes in the style of church and fellowship life over the past few years has been a renewed emphasis on praise and worship. This is seen as much more than singing songs together, it is a heart cry to God and expresses the reality of our feelings towards him. Ironically, many children and young people in the church nowadays seem to be almost totally switched off to all this. In the meetings they can be observed looking out of the window, looking around at others, looking at their watches, looking bored!

Sometimes, of course, they have every right to be bored because we have done nothing to make it interesting. I can remember as a child working out the half way point in the hymn and trying to estimate the exact number of minutes until we would all sit down again! Then for us as children it was a few action songs in Sunday school. The songs were normally exactly the same ones that our parents – and even grandparents – sang when they were young. All the old favourites such as "Deep and wide", "The wise man built his house upon the rock" and "Jesus bids us shine" were regularly given an airing! A little later newer songs began to emerge such as "From the rising of the sun" and "Thank you, Jesus". History is beginning to repeat itself as at least in some circles we are still dusting off these old faithfuls week by week.

In an age where God is renewing us in praise and worship we must somehow find a way to bridge the vast gap between where the adults are and where the children and young people are.

The answer does not lie in devising a new action song. The key is in seeing children and young people having a real experience of God in their lives so that praise and worship take on a whole new reality and meaning for them.

It is not true that young people just need an action song in order for praise and worship to be suitable for them. Few adults and very few leaders seem to believe that children have a real capacity for genuine worship. I am not against action songs – I have written several and use them regularly. What I am against is the idea that action songs are the be-all and end-all of a child's spiritual experience.

What do we mean by praise and worship?
The term praise and worship is widely used. It is part of our church experience. International conferences are organised to discuss it. It is part of our Kingdom culture. But what does it all mean? Is "praise" fast and bouncy, frothy and frivolous? Is "worship" quiet and contemplative, heavy and miserable? Does it have very much to do with singing songs at all?

The classic analysis of praise and worship in a meeting context goes something like this. We arrive and start off by singing a few fast, bouncy songs to blow away the cobwebs. Then we move into quieter more contemplative songs to draw near to God. The idea is based around the Old Testament temple concept. Here the idea was that we enter his gates with thanksgiving, his courts with praise, but then go on to worship in the Holy of Holies. This analysis sees praise as a precursor to worship, a sort of spiritual warm-up for the real business which is to be quiet and contemplative.

I believe the Holy of Holies is not some form of spiritual Utopia which we must strive to reach in our meetings. Rather it is a dimension we are already living in without having to struggle to achieve it. It is an issue which affects our whole lives not just the meetings. In fact my experience has been that sometimes the meetings can actually dampen worship! Many is the time I have gone to a meeting bright and happy but gone home depressed and miserable!

We must not lose sight of the fact that in one sense we have been living in the Holy of Holies since the day we became Christians. From that day our lives were "hidden with Christ in God" (Colossians 3:3). Whilst it is true that there is a progression in the Christian life in terms of maturity and holiness, we were actually transferred into a different Kingdom the day we became Christians.

So many Christians have built up a theology of struggling and striving for achievement in the Kingdom of God. This is as true of worship as it is in other areas. I believe this to be a misguided and unbiblical perspective. Our Kingdom culture is shot through with this kind of thinking that basically says, "I have to try hard to make it in the Kingdom." For example, we often hear phrases such as "As we seek your face" as though God is remote and we have to struggle to gain his attention! Another is "As we come into your presence . . ." Whenever I hear that phrase it makes me want to ask, "And where have you been all week?" It is a small illustration but it indicates that in our thinking the meeting is the special place to encounter God, and we must try hard in the meeting to make it work now that we have come aside from the world and are in "God's house".

The Church is a collection of redeemed people. It is not a building. Neither have we come aside from the world. We tend to think that there is a sharp divide between the secular and spiritual. The truth is that God was with us on Saturday at our picnic just as much as he is with us on Sunday at our 10.30am church meeting!

When it comes to praise and worship we tend to think in a similar way. We tend to struggle and strive in an effort to please God. We think we have to be very quiet and reverent. In the quiet our worship can easily become heavy and miserable and we kid ourselves if we think we are somehow breaking through.

It is my belief that God wants us to break down the rigid wall we have built between praise on the one hand and worship on the other. We need to worship God in our praise and praise God in our worship. Praise and worship are not so much something we do, i.e. songs we sing. Rather, they are a lifestyle, something we *are* which affects what we do. In our praise and worship we need to develop flexibility so that we can go from fast to slow then back again, then stop for a prophetic word, for example, and generally flow together in it. The idea of fast always moving into slow will lead us into set formats and we shall be in danger of falling into "religion".

Praise and worship are for the whole family. It is not necessary to reach a certain age or spiritual maturity first. I have enjoyed some wonderful times with Spirit-filled children leading them in worship. One of the most emotional sights for me is to see children filled with the Holy Spirit and worshipping God with smiles on their young faces, hands in the air adoring their Lord! What a tragedy that I never really understood worship until I was an adult. Instead all I knew was an old-fashioned Sunday school approach which today is about as relevant as roast beef in a vegetarian restaurant! Although it was probably not out of place then, the sad fact is that so often the approach has remained exactly the same even though life has moved on.

Freedom in praise and worship
There is a great need for God's people to be released in praise and worship. We can sing all the latest songs, we can do all the actions like putting our hands in the air or falling over(!), but if we are not truly released in our own spirits we will be concentrating on the externals rather than on worshipping God.

It amazes me on my travels, especially in this country, that in spite of all the emphasis on praise and worship and in spite of all the resources and materials available, many Christians are still not free in their praise and worship. If we are not free our children will not be free. Just this week I had a letter from a church inviting me to lead various sessions for adults, children and the whole family. A footnote to the booking form reads: "Significant number of adults not into fun-style worship or lively worship. Gifts of Spirit not used in worship at the moment."

So where are we in Britain at the moment? Thankfully there are many churches and fellowships that are into Spirit-filled worship and are developing this, but many have not even begun to experience a personal and corporate breakthrough in this area.

As has been already noted, it seems that joy and enthusiasm are out of vogue. Heaviness and apathy are in. But the Kingdom is not about being miserable but about being happy! Some of us may sometimes feel that we have had problems, difficulties, a bad week, hurts and so on which justify our being miserable in our worship. But if we are saying that worshipping our God is hard and makes no difference to our circumstances, then what kind of a God do we serve? What sort of advertisement is it if we are effectively saying, "Become a Christian then you can be like me and opt out from worshipping someone who makes no difference to my life anyway."

The question is this: Is it really any wonder that our children are so often bound up and switched off when it comes to praise and worship? Are we showing a powerful lifestyle of praise and worship even in the thick of all our problems?

The Church in our generation is not unique in experiencing these kind of problems. Paul wrote to the Galatians probably in AD 48 or 49 and said, "It is for freedom that Christ has set us free. Stand firm then and do not let yourselves be burdened again by a yoke of slavery'' (chapter 5:1). Although Christ had come to set them free from the curse of the Law, already – only twenty or so years after the Church was launched in power at Pentecost – they were beginning to get back into bondage. So quickly the freedom and power were in danger of evaporating. Some of those in the Church would have actually been around personally twenty years or so earlier. How quickly pioneers in one generation can become settlers in another.

My travels have taken me into many denominational churches. Here especially there is a need for freedom in praise and worship at all levels. One church I was in recently said that they have drums, bass, keyboard and electric guitars once every two weeks. The other week they have the traditional organ. What they were really saying was that they did not want to go wholeheartedly into something new. They wanted to try to please everybody. Where is the leadership in all this? When we try to keep everyone happy we end up keeping no one happy.

Much of my work has also been in what used to be called ''house churches'' or what are now called the newer churches. I have found many individual fellowships where praise and worship are a real struggle and where there is as much need of freedom as in many denominational churches.

In the Old Testament we read of a number of occasions when God's people did not hold back in their worship. One of the best known is when David brought the Ark back into its rightful place, the city of Jerusalem, and danced before the Lord. Even though he was despised by his own wife he pressed on and continued to worship God (2 Samuel 6:14–16). As God establishes his Kingdom in its rightful place we need to be prepared to be released in our worship even if others around despise us.

When churches are in unity and are prepared to press

forward together in praise and worship we can expect big changes and blessing. In 2 Chronicles 5:13ff we read that when the Ark was returned to the Temple, "The trumpeters and singers joined in unison, as with one voice, to give praise and thanks to the Lord. Accompanied by trumpets, cymbals and other instruments, they raised their voices in praise to the Lord and sang: 'He is good; his love endures for ever.' Then the temple of the Lord was filled with a cloud, and the priests could not perform their service because of the cloud, for the glory of the Lord filled the temple of God." How amazing!

Also well known is Psalm 150 which encourages us to praise the Lord with all that we have and to give everything in our worship of God. And we must, of course, involve our children in this. It is not only good sense and logical, it is also very scriptural.

For example, when Nehemiah had finished building the city walls he dedicated them to God with a lavish party of praise and worship. Nehemiah 12:43 says, "And on that day they offered great sacrifices, rejoicing because God had given them great joy. The women and children also rejoiced. The sound of rejoicing in Jerusalem could be heard far away."

What a significant day it will be in our own land when the sound of families praising God together will be heard far away and will affect the communities around us! If all this was possible under the old covenant, how much more joyful should be the praise and worship from us who are under the new covenant, and filled with the power of the Holy Spirit as well!

We have such a responsibility to lead our children into freedom in praise and worship. One of the saddest events I ever witnessed was at a national evangelistic outreach programme in Wales. I was leading two celebration events for children at a sports hall on a Saturday. Nearly 1,000 attended and "rocked along with Rich" in praise and worship. It was a great time and obviously a new dimension for many – adults and children alike. When it came to the teaching I gave a simple evangelistic word and 140 came forward to become Christians. Whilst the counselling was going on many church people appeared and dragged the children off to the waiting coaches. Any literature with a contact address was confiscated and torn up. These children who a few moments before and for the first time were freely worshipping God – and many who had just given their lives to Jesus – were immediately warned against this "extreme form of religion" by chapel people, and bussed home. I felt devastated not only because my own approach had been rejected but because my heart went out to those children as I wondered how their faith would survive. Adult leaders can either encourage children into more of God or put them back years.

One church I went to recently asked if I could do my usual high-energy celebration session in an evangelistic context, but then asked if I could considerably moderate the approach for "church" twelve hours later on the Sunday morning. In other words, they wanted it lively for the sinners and miserable for the saints! Surely our children deserve more than this. We need to show our children a consistency of approach in praise and worship, otherwise we are little better than the radio evangelists of yesteryear who preached on the airwaves and expected people to become Christians and then throw their radios away!

Characteristics of praise and worship

Praise and worship is not an activity, it is a lifestyle. It is much more than just singing songs—it has to do with the whole strategy of the Kingdom of God. It is strategic because it is powerful and reminds us that we are all in a spiritual war. Praise and worship are actually part of our armoury as Christians in spiritual warfare. If children are involved in an environment of healthy praise and worship they will actually be better equipped to stand against Satan – without even realising it!

There is a lot which could be said on this subject but we shall consider three basic aspects.

1. Praise and worship reveal lifestyle deficiencies
We cannot live carelessly all week, pleasing ourselves, and then expect to contribute to a dynamic expression of praise and worship on a Sunday. If our lives are lukewarm during the week we cannot expect to throw a spiritual switch at 10.30 on Sunday morning and expect to be red hot! For a couple of hours on a Sunday church in this context is simply a corporate reflection of our lives as individuals over the other 166 hours in the week.

One reason why some people cannot cope with enthusiasm and joy in worship is because their lives are not up to it. It is easier to retreat into the safety of "true worship", by which we mean simply quietness, as it will make no demands on our lives. We can more easily opt out without anyone else noticing!

I have even known people opt for teaching in Sunday school or creche because they cannot cope with praise and worship. They think that other people will not recognise their true motives—that all they are doing is escaping! In fact they might think they deserve a pat on the back for being prepared to work with the children rather than sit in the meeting! What they do not realise is the harm they are doing in the lives of the most impressionable sector of the church – the children. How ironic that so often leaders allow this to happen.

It is easy to confuse quietness and spirituality. It is a misconception to think that if we want to be really spiritual we must be really quiet and miserable! I have been in meetings where we have all waited quietly for something to happen only to find out later that nothing did! My years in the Brethren taught me that there is no virtue in quietness

per se. Only quietness initiated by the Holy Spirit to do
something specific is acceptable. I have found that a people
praising God with all they are and all they have, giving out
in worship rather than seated quietly like marble statues,
is far more likely to result in the demonstrable presence of
the Holy Spirit doing his work.

Only this last Sunday at my home fellowship (and
quite rarely for me) I was literally in tears as the Holy
Spirit began to deal with me and speak to me. All around
people of all ages were out of their seats worshipping
God but in the midst of it all God was at work in a powerful
way.

What is sometimes called "worship" is often nothing more
than heaviness dressed up to sound spiritual. Those who
like it that way are often fearful of what would happen if
they were really to let go. Some know that their lives would
not bear exposure to a freer approach.

The answer is not to moderate our approach to worship.
That merely masks the issue. The solution lies in getting
our own lives sorted out so that we can move on together
into new realms of worship. We need to be a radical people,
rising to the challenge and seeing our lives changed to be
able to worship our God, alongside our children, in Spirit
and in truth.

2. Praise and worship stir up the powers of Darkness

Of course merely singing what we used to call "choruses"
never stirs up spiritual opposition. We are talking here about
our hearts and lives being in gear before we engage our
mouths in worship. I have met those who say that stirring
up the powers of darkness sounds dangerous and that it
would be better not to tread that route just in case something
goes wrong. This is exactly what Satan wants us to think.
We need to recognise that Jesus has already won the victory
for us and that, as Paul reminded the Corinthian church,
" . . . the weapons we fight with are not the weapons of

the world. On the contrary they have divine power to demolish strongholds'' (2 Corinthians 10:4).

I have occasionally been leading meetings when someone begins to act peculiarly and begins to manifest satanic influence that has to be prayed out. The fact that this sometimes happens during praise and worship suggests that when real worship is going on it stirs up the powers of darkness. It is interesting that the very first incident recorded about Jesus' ministry is that he went into the *synagogue* at Capernaum and there had to cast out an unclean spirit in the meeting (Mark 1:21–28). There is often a reaction when the power of God comes down.

We have been called to victory. Although some have become triumphalistic and unreal the fact remains that we are a people of victory – even when everything is going wrong! Praise and worship help us to assert the victory because as well as reaching out to God it also tells Satan that we are not going to allow our circumstances to rob God of the worship and praise which belong to him.

3. *Praise and worship actually release Satan's hold*

A story that is often presented to children is the capture of Jericho, told in Joshua chapter 6. Amazingly Joshua sent the spiritual leaders to the front line to blow the trumpets. The trained soldiers were behind. The command for action was simply the blowing of the trumpet. On the seventh lap when the trumpet was sounded Joshua commanded the people to shout and as they shouted out the walls came down.

It was the same strategy that God later gave to Abijah, king of Judah. In 2 Chronicles 13:14–15 we read, ''The priests blew their trumpets and the men of Judah raised the battle cry. At the sound of their battle cry God routed Jeroboam and all Israel before Abijah and Judah.''

Similarly in 2 Chronicles 20 we read how Jehoshaphat was able to defeat Moab and Ammon. He started off by praying and interceding. Interestingly the "wives, children and little ones stood there before the Lord" (verse 13) with him. Then God spoke prophetically into the situation, assured them of victory and told Jehoshaphat how he should prepare. He was told to put people in the front line who could sing and praise! As they were obedient the Lord set ambushes against the enemy who were then defeated. No wonder that after plundering they went into the temple with harps, lutes and trumpets (verses 21, 22 and 28)!

"Our struggle is not against flesh and blood but against the rulers, against the authorities, against the powers of this dark world and against the spiritual forces of evil in the heavenly realms" (Ephesians 6:12). Praise and worship are one means by which the whole family of the church, adults, youth and children, can withstand the evil one.

Getting into the reality of the revelation

It is one thing to know we need to make progress in praise and worship in our church family, it is another thing to do it!

In my Brethren background the ethos and style was that to show emotions means weakness and shallowness. When confronted with an entirely new approach I found it difficult to cope.

Once filled with the Spirit I really wanted to join with others in clapping but found it difficult. I was fourteen at the time and it is clear to me now that the church environment I had experienced as a child was responsible for the way I was then feeling as a teenager.

Gradually I broke through the clapping barrier – only to find myself confronted by a new barrier! I noticed that people around me were lifting their hands in worship. I thought I would never be able to do that. I started in a small way be raising my hand cautiously beside my hymnbook. I reasoned that if anyone appeared to have noticed I could easily convert it into a scratch on the cheek! But I knew I had to break through the barrier. When I boldly stuck my hand our I felt so self-conscious and embarrassed that I was convinced everyone in the whole meeting had stopped worshipping and all eyes were looking at me.

After that I soon encountered another problem – dancing. This was the most difficult for me to conquer. I thought up every argument I could and even tried to convince myself that I was free not to have to dance! The truth is of course that I was not free to dance and that was the issue. Deep down I knew that things had to change but I fought this more than all the others put together.

The occasion that turned my barrier into a frontier came quite unexpectedly. Whilst on holiday cruising on the Thames we stopped at Oxford where an American team called the Maranatha Praise Band happened to be doing some concerts. I went one evening to the Randolph Hotel where the meetings were held. It was a very powerful time of praise and worship and everyone was really getting into it. As a non-dancer I felt rather conspicuous. This, I decided, was going to be my big moment. As I started to jig up and down I was immediately conscious of feeling very embarrassed. I felt awkward but it really did not seem to matter as I was caught up in praising my God. As that was only the first occasion I had of course to persevere and carry on. Soon I found that I was genuinely free in this area and only when I had reached that stage was I truly free not to dance. Until then I had no freedom to choose because I knew that to exercise a choice one must have two options. As a non-dancer I had only one option – not to dance – and so had no real choice at all!

As I see others released in praise and worship I find that dancing is still the biggest hurdle. Even with children many have seen that dancing has been unacceptable in their church for so long that it can take a little time for them to break free. For adults, of course, it can be even worse. One slightly amusing thing I have noticed is this: if people are asked to clap along they generally will do so. Similarly if people are asked to raise their hands in worship they generally will. But if they are asked to dance, immediately they refuse saying it is not in the Spirit. What is the difference? The issue is not really whether it is in the Spirit or not, it is the fact that they are not free. Ask a free person to dance and there is no problem! We are very good at putting up smokescreens in the Church to cover over the real issues. We need to make sure that we are honest in our praise and worship and allow God to challenge us to progress, whatever age we are. Of course dancing does not in itself make for spiritual progress. Dancing is a by-product of the new-found freedom that God is bringing the Church into at the close of the twentieth century.

Involving our children

Children do not have to be restricted to the action song only, but can be strategically involved in worshipping with us. But to involve our children we must be involved ourselves. To illustrate the power of children in worship we can do no better than to close with the words of Matthew 21:15–17:

> But when the chief priests and the teachers of the law saw the wonderful things he did and the *children* shouting in the temple area, "Hosanna to the Son of David," they were indignant.
>
> "Do you hear what these children are saying?" they asked him.
>
> "Yes," replied Jesus, "have you never read, 'From the lips of children and infants you have ordained praise'?" And he left them and went out of the city to Bethany, where he spent the night.

Chapter 13

Healing

It is a historical fact that whenever God initiates any form of renewal it is normally accompanied by a new emphasis on healing. It is therefore no surprise that over the last twenty-five years or so, much has been said and written about this very important subject. The whole emphasis of this book is that we need to see renewal, restoration and revival taking place amongst the sector of the church that comprises children. Healing is therefore an important issue in the context of children in the church.

Before we can effectively equip our children in this area we need to feel confident in it ourselves. There has been a lot of nonsense talked about healing and a lot of superficial unreality. But behind all this is a loving God who wants his people to be well and who wants to lead us into the experience of what many know only in theory.

There is a great need to be honest when it comes to healing. We have to be mature enough to admit that sometimes people are not healed when we pray for them. We must not fall into some kind of super-spiritual self-protection syndrome and blame the person being prayed for, saying, for example, that it is their fault they are not healed because they did not have enough faith! Sometimes this may be the case but very often it will not.

Healing is a complex issue that we do not really understand. Sometimes people are healed immediately, sometimes they are healed gradually and sometimes they are not healed at all. I have learned not to allow what I do not understand to affect what I do understand. I continue to pray for the sick and encourage children to do the same.

I would rather pray for one hundred people and see only two people healed than pray for no one and see nothing happen. Then if I can see the percentages change so that five and then ten are healed, I shall be making real progress.

Two extreme views

There are two groups of people with two extreme views that we need to be wary about. The first is the "name it claim it" brigade who seem to feel that somehow God exists for their benefit. They feel justified in acting like spoilt children in demanding things from God. Their view is that as Christians we have a divine right to health, wealth, healing and happiness! It sounds great – and is particularly appealing to twentieth-century people who may be very happy to work a bit of materialism into their theology. The truth is that life is not like that. It does not always work out the way we would like. This view leads to disappointment and disillusionment.

At the opposite extreme, some people have no faith whatever for healing. They may have had a bad experience with healing teaching in the past and have now thrown the baby out with the bath water. What is worse they have become suspicious and over-cautious about the whole issue. Such negative attitudes do not produce faith. I have hardly ever seen negative and critical people being used by God in areas such as healing. Negativism and pessimism are not the route to lead our children into an exciting adventure of faith when it comes to healing. Believe it or not I have even met people who actually hope that people will not be healed when they pray so that their own negative view can be shown to have been "right" after all and so that they can say, "There, I told you so . . . I've seen it all before."

If anything I would rather err on the side of the prosperity brigade because at least they may see things happen!

Healing in the Old Testament

Healing is not new. Right back in the Old Testament we find the issues of sickness and healing being brought into sharp focus.

In Numbers 21:8–9 we read all about Moses' bronze snake set up on a pole. God's people had been bitten by the snakes God sent as a punishment against the rebellious Israelites. When they ran to Moses and repented they were still suffering from fatal snake bites. "The Lord said to Moses, 'Make a snake and put it up on a pole; anyone who is bitten can look at it and live.' So Moses made a bronze snake and put it up on a pole. Then when anyone was bitten by a snake and looked at the bronze snake, he lived." Although this clearly foreshadows Jesus and his plan to rescue mankind from spiritual death, it remains literally true as well. When the Israelites looked on the snake they were healed.

Later on in 2 Samuel 12:15 it is clear that David believed in a God of healing even though it did not quite work out as he may have hoped! After the affair with Bathsheba resulting in her pregnancy, the child was born but was sick. "David pleaded with God for the child. He fasted and went into his house and spent the nights lying on the ground. The elders of his household stood beside him to get him up from the ground, but he refused, and he would not eat any food with them. On the seventh day the child died" (verses 16–18). Clearly David believed God could do it and believed it could even happen in his situation. The fact that healing did not in the event take place in no way detracts from the fact that David believed in a God who healed.

Elijah is well known for his Old Testament signs and wonders ministry. When the son of the widow of Zarephath became ill and grew worse and worse until finally he stopped breathing, Elijah stretched the boy out on his own bed and prayed for him. Miraculously he was raised from the dead (see 1 Kings 17:7–24).

Elisha also had a healing ministry. The Shunammite's son,

whose conception Elisha had prayed for, was now ill (2 Kings 4). A servant had carried him in from working with his father in the field. The boy was complaining of a bad headache. Whilst he was sitting on his mother's lap, he died. After some spiritual mouth-to-mouth resuscitation he sneezed and got up perfectly well.

Hezekiah came face to face with a God of healing. He had received a prophetic word that he was going to die. He prayed and prayed about this and wept bitterly. Then the prophet came with the good news that God would heal him, add fifteen years to his life and deliver his enemies into his hands (2 Kings 20:1–6).

God showed himself to be interested in his people long before New Testament times. He revealed part of his unchanging character that, as a general principle, he wants his people healed.

Healing in the New Testament

In the New Testament we move onto more familiar territory! In all the accounts of the healing miracles of Jesus, one important fact emerges: there is no blueprint, no formula for success. It seems that Jesus treated people as individuals and his approach therefore varied from person to person according to their specific needs. Sometimes however he did not even deal with individuals but healed whole crowds of anything they had wrong with them (see for example Matthew 4:24 and 8:16).

Often faith was required for healing (see Luke 7:1–10), but sometimes it was not required at all (see Luke 13:10–13). Sometimes Jesus simply had compassion on those he saw around him and healed them (see Matthew 14:14). Sometimes Jesus spoke a word (see Mark 7:34 and Luke 5:13), at other times he said nothing (see Mark 5:27–29).

Two things in particular strike me about healing in the New Testament:

1. *Healing and evangelism*

It seems that Jesus healed almost exclusively people who were outside the Kingdom. We do not read that he spent time dealing with his disciples' illnesses. We read very little about healing in the early church other than in an evangelistic context. Perhaps the reason for this is that as God's people we need to be in faith for health rather than healing, for prevention rather then cure.

The fact that Jesus healed many non-Christians does not mean that there is no place for healing amongst Christians. In fact our friends provide us with a very good practising ground before we are let loose on those outside the Kingdom! Certainly in Scripture we find that Epaphrodites, a co-worker with Paul, was sick and very nearly died but God healed him (see Phillippians 2:27). James 5:14–15 says, "Is there any one of you [i.e. Christians] sick? He should call the elders of the church to pray over him and anoint him with oil in the name of the Lord. And the prayer offered in faith will make the sick person well; the Lord will raise him up."

2. *Not everyone was healed immediately*

Reference has already been made to David's child who died. Paul's trainee Timothy was often not exactly the picture of health. In fact Paul had to tell him to drink a little wine because of his stomach "and your frequent illnesses" (1 Timothy 5:23). Also we read of Trophimus (one of Paul's team who was left sick in Miletus (2 Timothy 4:20).

Although we need to bear in mind these instances, we are not to look at all the times when it did not seem to happen in a negative way. We are called to press on in healing and to see the sick raised up, even if it does not always work out in the way we would like.

Understanding the root of sickness

Illness occurs for a variety of different reasons. It is helpful to distinguish between them so that we can pray specifically.

Healing

1. Demonic activity

Although sickness is the result of the fall and therefore an activity of Satan, I do not believe that all sickness is therefore demonic. Sometimes Jesus cast out a spirit of infirmity but more often he simply told the ill person to get better. In some cases, however, sickness can be the direct result of demonic activity. Often the hallmarks of this are sporadic illnesses for no apparent reason which may have no real medical cause. A discernment of spirits is necessary to work out whether the cause is demonic or not.

I normally start off by assuming no demonic activity. If then while I am praying I get a sense in my spirit, a sort of spiritual gut-feeling, that there is demonic oppression behind the sickness I will deal with it as a deliverance. To put this in context it is very rare in my experience for the illness to have direct demonic roots. It is, however, more common in people who have dabbled in the occult.

2. Lifestyle

Soon after I left my job and began to travel on a full-time basis an interesting thing began to happen. Fairly regularly, every few months, I would get ill. I would have a temperature and have all the symptoms of flu. When Lynda and I prayed against it nothing happened. It was almost as though it was a bug which had built up a resistance to prayer! Then one morning I woke up with a severe pain in my chest and had to go straight to the doctor. He told me it was nothing serious but that I was overdoing it. The periodic illnesses were stress. My body was shouting "Enough!" and forcing me to rest.

The root of the problem was not sickness but stress caused by my lifestyle. I realised that I could not ask God to heal me from what was in effect a lifestyle problem that was entirely within my power to curb. The reason for this was simply that if I was healed I would carry on exactly the same as before!

3. *Specific issues*

There are times when specific issues can prevent us from receiving healing. Sin, bitterness, hatred, resentment and so on can be relevant here. However we must be careful at this point. It is only too easy to go deep sea fishing in our lives and become inward-looking and heavy, trying desperately to dredge up some sin or problem. I am a great believer in assuming that there are no such issues. If there are I would expect that God would make them apparent without the need for us to do a lot of heavy digging.

One danger to watch out for is the claim that sickness has been allowed by God to teach people a spiritual lesson. This is fine in principle but the problem is that these same people are usually busy taking all sorts of medication to get better! If the illness is genuinely of the Lord, why resist him by taking medication so as to get better? If it is not of the Lord why not be honest and admit it?

4. *Mere illness*

Sometimes we simply get ill. I hope I never get super-spiritual about healing. If I get a headache after travelling many hours in a hot car, I simply take a tablet. There is nothing wrong with that if we believe that God has given us the medicine in the first place and that it is he who heals us in any event. Once I was arguing this point with a lady who told me that all tablets are wrong and it is a lack of faith to take them. The problem was that when someone else said she had a sore throat this lady handed her a throat sweet!

It is a medical fact that bodies tend to wear out with age. Ridiculously enough, at my age, a few tiny hairs have even been observed trying to escape from my head! When praying for an older person I normally pray for them to be restored according to their years. It may be unreal to expect God to heal granddad and then for him thereafter to have the physique of Superman!

Faith

Faith is a very important issue in healing, but it is so often misunderstood. The reason – or excuse – given when people are not healed has often been that they did not have enough faith. This provided the person praying with a convenient escape route. The problem was that it also added a sense of guilt and failure to the person being prayed for which often did untold damage.

I find this kind of analysis quite unacceptable. Faith is not something to be striven for or struggled into, it is rather a response to a word which God has spoken to us. First comes the voice of God (a *rhema* word to us individually) and in response to that word comes our faith. It is vital we understand this. As has already been noted, God first told Abraham to go into the desert away from all that was familiar. Then Abraham responded to the word and did it (Genesis 12:1). First the word and then the response of faith. Similarly with Noah, God spoke a strange word to build a massive boat nearly half the size of the QE2 in his back garden miles away from any water. Noah heard the word and responded in faith. Also with Peter. He was able to step out and walk on water only because God had told him to do it first. Jesus had said, "Come" (Matthew 14:29).

These and many other examples serve to illustrate Romans 10:17: "*Faith* comes by hearing the message and the message is heard *through the word* of Christ." The word must precede action. That is why the words of Hebrews 11:1 are so true, that "Faith is the substance [i.e. the sub-stance, something you are standing on] of things hoped for, the evidence of things not seen" (NKJV).

Faith must be understood in this context when it comes to healing. If we have received a specific and direct personal word that we will be healed, we can claim it. If God has spoken, we can act. It is not enough to claim general biblical promises blindly. We cannot walk on water on the basis of Peter's experience which is recorded in the Bible. In the same way we cannot claim anything other than a specific word from the Lord to us if we are going to be sure of our healing.

I feel strongly about people's tendency to rush in and pray without thinking and without first trying to discern what God actually wants to say about healing. Jesus was a hundred per cent successful because he is God. He only did what he knew his Father was doing. If we went a little more slowly and used more discernment maybe our praying would be more targeted and therefore more successful. To hear from God may sometimes require prayer and fasting. Often we are not prepared for long-term commitment of this kind. If we do not get what we want straight away we tend to move on to the next person.

When the disciples could not deliver a boy from demonic activity resulting in sickness, Jesus explained that this kind does not go out except by prayer and fasting (Matthew 17:14–21). The point Jesus was making was that a quick, cheap prayer is often not enough. Long-term commitment in terms of prayer and fasting may well be necessary. This is an aspect of healing which is not often talked about. However, my own experience would certainly confirm this. For example, on one occasion a lady in my housegroup was taken seriously ill with a brain haemorrhage. As a group we began to fast and pray. Sometimes we would meet literally in the middle of the night to pray if some specific news was received from the hospital.

As we continued with it (and it did not happen straight away) God began to speak into the situation. Scriptures, prophecies and words of knowledge were all given indicating that she would be healed. There was a general rise of faith. Then the news came from the hospital that nothing further could be done and that it was only a matter of time before she would die. Even though, humanly, death seemed inevitable, we decided to believe what God was saying rather that the circumstances facing us. A few days later she was miraculously healed in hospital to the total amazement of all the doctors and hospital staff. To us the main lesson in all this was the long-term commitment to fast, pray and see it through.

When can we believe for healing?
We can have faith for healing when God has spoken into our situation with a personal word as already outlined.

We can also believe for healing when we receive a gift of faith. This is one of the gifts of the Holy Spirit which is available to us. An example happened recently when I had just finished preaching. A man came running up asking me to pray for healing for his back. Before I could say anything God gave me a gift of faith. I knew that I could pray in confidence for healing. It was as though I had been given a green light from the Lord. I knew it was right. I prayed and the man said he felt an immediate improvement and knew that he was healed.

The other time we can believe for healing is when we receive a word of knowledge. I have known many occasions when people are healed as a result of this. Recent personal examples include spine disorders, stomach problems, medical back conditions, skin complaints and other more minor ailments. There is no reason at all why children cannot be involved in this. If they are filled with the Spirit and taught about words of knowledge by leaders who use these gifts themselves, children will flourish in them. I positively encourage this and have seen many specific healings take place as a result of words of knowledge among children.

Sometimes of course God will act in a sovereign way out of love and compassion. In spite of our having no faith, no word to claim, God will do it anyway!

A general feeling of expectancy is important. I find in taking meetings that when the ministry team, the local organisers and the individual members of the congregation or audience are expecting great things it helps a great deal. There is nothing like a miserable atmosphere to dampen enthusiasm. I have led meetings where it is like trying to light a damp bonfire! Even Jesus encountered this in his own home town of Nazareth: "He could not do any miracles there except lay hands on a few sick people and heal them. And he was amazed at their lack of faith [or expectancy]" (Mark 6:5–6).

Getting personally involved

For me the road to understanding healing has been a long and perplexing route. I am still travelling! I have had to gain some experience myself before being equipped to share it with children. There was a time when I thought I could never be used in healing. I used to hide behind the excuse that perhaps it was not my gift. That gave me the justification I needed to do nothing! The joke used to be that if I prayed for someone to be healed they would probably get worse – so it was better not to pray in the first place! Nowadays I am prepared to try. I would love to be able to say that everyone is always healed instantly when I pray, but it is not true. What I have found though is that as I operate according to words of knowledge, a gift of faith or in response to a specific word from God (it does not matter who receives this provided *someone* does!), healing takes place more often.

The first time I prayed for someone to be healed was when a friend turned round to me in a meeting and asked me to pray for a long-standing sinus problem. I did not have a clue what to do so I prayed very simply as a child would. Immediately he was healed and had no further trouble. I could hardly believe it! From then on my new-found ministry went downhill and it seemed that nothing happened when I prayed. As God began to show me the importance of knowing his mind on the particular illness I began to do less general praying and to spend more time finding out what God was saying about individual situations before praying for healing.

As I began learning for myself I decided to start sharing it with children who, after all, tend to have less inhibitions than adults.

The first occasion I put it to the test with children was when I was leading children's celebration sessions at Eurofire, an international conference at the NEC. One morning I felt we should cover the subject of healing in the main teaching that evening. I announced it, the children got excited, the team looked nervous and I knew I was stuck with it! That evening as I looked round from the stage I thought I had never seen a more healthy looking bunch than this! And here I was about to cover healing. I swallowed hard and went for it.

After the teaching I gave a simple appeal and the first person to respond was a girl aged ten. She was wearing specially designed glasses because the doctors had said that in the space of three to five years she would be totally blind. I had been hoping for someone with a cold, not someone with a serious eyesight problem! I got the children involved and together we prayed. Immediately she keeled over and her glasses fell off. When we had finished praying for her she started to get up and began to shout out loud "I can see! I can see!" I nearly fell over in amazement as she said it was the first time for years she had been able to see anything at all without her glasses.

In the same meeting many other wonderful healings took place. One of the team was healed of total deafness in one ear and had no need for her hearing aid. Several were healed of asthma and were handing in an interesting collection of inhalers! And all of this was taking place in the children's meetings.

Shortly after this conference I was leading a very small event, a church week away in Kent. Would similar things happen in a small, local context? I was determined not to see the power of God relegated to the large conference only. The stuff of the Kingdom is the ordinary, everyday local situation. Here again some wonderful things happened. One boy was healed of having eyes which went in opposite directions. More inhalers were handed in as asthma was healed and many lives were healed from emotional as well as physical problems. One boy ran up to me and said "Listen!" I told him I could not hear anything and he said, "Isn't it great! My breathing used to sound like a tractor but now God has completely healed me!"

Sometimes parents have come to me after a meeting literally in tears telling of how God has powerfully healed their children. It is clear that God is doing wonderful things with children wherever we as adults give him the opportunity.

At a recent event we prayed for many children to be healed. The ministry was done almost exclusively by word of knowledge and my whole team was involved in this. For many of them I know it was a stretch of faith but it was rewarded when they received words and were linked up with the relevant child to pray together. The two main complaints to be healed were asthma and eczema. Children were showing each other where the spots had been and were busy comparing arms and legs! One young boy jumped up onto the stage and showed the whole meeting his clean white arms that only the previous day had been covered in eczema especially at the joints.

Teaching children about healing
Obviously healing has to be made simple for children to understand. It is important to have an air of expectancy and anticipation in the meeting. All the leaders must be united about it. A few half-hearted leaders with no personal experience who are cautious and suspicious and who want to build an escape route for themselves in case nothing happens will not be disappointed when nothing does happen!

The approach I often use is to ask the children to close their eyes and ask God if he wants to begin to heal them. Some children will say yes, others will say no and some will not be sure. I will always pray with those who say yes and will stand with them in their belief that God is giving them the green light. Although I would normally pray in general terms for those with the amber and red lights I will not pray authoritatively for their healing.

Teaching children about timescale is important. Sometimes people will be healed immediately, sometimes it will be a gradual process. Even when it is a gradual process we need to believe that God is still at work. Gradual healing is not a cop-out for when nothing happens instantaneously. The illustration I often use is the difference between an electric light and an electric kettle. As soon as a light is switched on there is instant light. On the other hand when an electric kettle is switched on it does not seem at first that anything has happened. The truth is, of course that the power is flowing—in fact more power is being consumed than with the light. If we come back a few minutes later the kettle will be boiling. In both cases the power was on from the beginning but in the case of the kettle the results are not quite so immediate.

Making it all happen

We shall never see our children encouraged to pray for healing unless we are prepared to launch out into it ourselves first. As we can only effectively teach from personal experience we must be developing personal experience even if we do not become experts.

Sometimes people have said to me that if God wants to bring children into healing he will just do it. Unfortunately this is simply not the case. It is a smokescreen. It is our job to actively desire it. As we make the first moves God will meet with us. He will never barge in uninvited to dump a load of healing on us. We have to request it. As it says in Matthew 7:7–8, ''Ask and it will be given to you; seek and you will find; knock and the door will be opened to you. For everyone who asks receives; he who seeks finds; and to him who knocks, the door will be opened.'' We must take the initiative.

As adults and especially as leaders we must not let fear, unanswered questions and the risk of failure stop us from leading our children into the fullness of the good news of the Kingdom. Who knows, we may well learn something from them! Certainly we must not fall into the trap of merely preaching healing – we must live it!

Chapter 14

Children's Leaders

Children's leaders are perhaps the most neglected sector of church leadership. Many children's leaders seem to be hardly even recognised let alone encouraged and valued. Churches sometimes show an anything-will-do attitude when it comes to appointing children's leaders.

The time has come to redress the balance – or, to put it more accurately, the imbalance.

At the same time there are, it has to be said, a lot of highly unsuitable people in children's leadership. These well-meaning people teach in an old-fashioned way using the methods of yesterday to convey a church ethos that is rapidly being swept away! I have come across many leaders who call themselves "Mr" Smith or "Mrs" Smith (as appropriate!), get even mature children to colour in Gospel Gem verses from the 1611 Authorised Version and for a special treat produce a musty old flannelgraph. As a very special treat older children may be shown a Fact and Faith film where they will see a nice clean young man with short back and sides, wearing a suit and driving a brand new Austin A40!

The time has come for a new breed of children's leader who will be properly recognised by church leadership and who will have a strategic rather than a peripheral role in the Kingdom of God.

There are a number of important aspects to children's leadership which need to be considered.

Discipleship models
Children are looking for heroes. They are looking for people on whom they can base their lives and their values. They

may not think about this consciously, but subconsciously it is the cry of every child.

Many leaders have opted out of this role. They think it sounds unspiritual. The thinking is that as leaders our lives should be like signposts pointing away from us and pointing towards God. But children live in the real world with real needs and are looking for role models. If we opt our of this, the children will still look for heroes. If they find none available in the Kingdom they will start to look outside it. Whilst I am by no means against rock stars, video heroes and so on, I do believe it is a tragedy when the leaders opt out of this frame and retreat into a sub-culture which is unrelated to the needs of children living in the real world.

Of course our lives as individuals need to be a suitable model. I have seen children's (and other) leaders' lives tainted with adultery, sin and lack of spirituality. Whilst none of us will ever be completely perfect we do need to recognise that we cannot kid children. They very quickly recognise it when things are not right. In any event, even if we could kid them we cannot kid God! If our lives are not right in major areas we may do untold damage in terms of shaping children's perceptions of right and wrong.

It goes without saying but it is vitally important that our leaders have had a real experience of Jesus. I come across denominational churches even today where it is not certain that the children's leaders have actually made a Christian commitment. It is futile to try to build anything on the sand.

Being relevant

The fact is that some children's leaders are simply not on the same wavelength as the children. Leaders must be able to communicate effectively with their children.

Communication involves both giving and receiving. We have to be able to give to the children; they have to be able to receive from us. It is a two-way process. And there are all sorts of barriers to communication.

The way we dress can be important. One of my favourite little sayings is this: You never get a second chance to create a first impression. If we look dowdy and old-fashioned we have already made a statement before we even open our mouths! The way we teach is also important. If we speak in a dreary monotone our style will cause the children to switch off even if the content of what we are saying is brilliant. A traditional manner can cause children to lose enthusiasm very quickly as they sense we are churning out the same old stuff the way it has always been churned out.

By contrast someone who is bright and cheerful, who is full of action and movement, prepared to make a fool of himself, gets the children laughing, and presents the teaching in a bright, fun way, is much more likely to communicate effectively.

I have seen leaders sitting on a chair whilst the children are on the floor, reading a story straight out of a book. The style is often very serious and a little patronising. On the other hand, I have seen others with a bit of personality, sitting (or standing) with the children and *telling* the story with imagination and enthusiasm. Without a doubt the latter approach is far more effective.

Communication comes from relationship. I find even on one-night events it is possible to gain the confidence and respect of children very quickly. Once the basic relationship is there they will be ready to receive what you have to say. Communication based on a remote, authoritarian, traditional approach will not work. We have to be friends with the children and earn their respect. That is why I never allow people to call me "Uncle Rich" or "Mr Hubbard", the whole idea makes me shudder! They call me Rich. Yet in many churches we still have "Aunties", "Uncles", "Sunday schools" and, worst of the lot, "Sunday school superintendents". I believe that true respect is earned. It does not come automatically by giving someone an "Auntie" badge.

With the greatest respect to older leaders who have been faithful for many years, I do believe that we need to see more young leaders in children's ministry. Younger people tend to be more in tune with the children, they talk the same language, wear the same clothes, and may communicate more naturally.

Age does not have too much to do with years, it has more to do with attitude and approach. Yet an older person who merely learns who is number one in the charts this week will not suddenly become a hit with the children, any more than a young trendy person will necessarily be successful merely by being young and trendy.

Ask some children's leaders about New Kids on the Block and you will probably be told about the nice young lads who have just moved into the neighbourhood! Ask some leaders about heroin and they may tell you about a brave young girl they know! Ask them about street-cred and they will probably think you are talking about dog's mess on the pavement! It sounds far fetched but it is not always too far from the truth. To be successful as leaders we must be relevant.

Taking the lead

Leaders must lead. This sounds rather obvious but it needs to be said. Some leaders in the church have become more like managers than leaders. We are not called to personnel management, we are called to leadership.

Going back to our signpost analogy, some children's leaders think it is enough if they stand at point A and simply point the way to B. The children (like adults) will never make it. They need to be led by someone who has already got there! Moses took the lead with the children of Israel in bringing them out of Egypt. Joshua took the lead in taking them in to the Promised Land. These men did not "lead" from Mission Control in Jerusalem, merely telling the people where to go. They were there with them, getting their hands dirty!

Whatever the issue with our children, we must take the lead if we really want to see them breaking through in new areas for themselves.

If for example, we want to see our children released in praise and worship we must first be free in it ourselves. I have seen people try and lead by telling children to clap yet not actually clapping themselves. I have seen leaders singing a song which talks about dancing but not actually dancing themselves and consequently not seeing the children dancing. In many church meetings I have observed leaders being completely switched off and totally bound up. It is obvious that they will never be able to lead in praise and worship until they have first come through on it for themselves.

Similarly if we really want to see children filled with the Holy Spirit and learning to use the gifts, we must lead by example. If our children see that we never worship in tongues or give prophecies, why should they? It is not enough to teach one thing but live another.

On many occasions I have led children's or youth meetings where leaders have been present but instead of joining in they have opted out. Instead of leaping around in the praise and worship, they are looking for a chair. Rather than being in amongst the people, they want to retreat to the back. Instead of entering into the programme, they want to chat among themselves. I have even had to stop a group of leaders from chatting amongst themselves while the main teaching was going on! Is it any wonder our children are so bound up when this is the kind of example we are giving them?

Ironically I have led ministry sessions where more work is done amongst the leaders than anyone else. Dealing with the leaders who are crying their hearts out as God is dealing with them is a very positive sign indeed.

There is a common misconception that older people are entitled to be completely switched off. I have found that it tends to be older people who are the most resistant to change and who tend to put themselves out less. I often find it irritating that approaches have to be modified for the older people. It is they who should be *giving* the lead! Younger people should be learning radical Christianity from them, not having to soft-pedal to try and keep them happy!

Thankfully I have found some older people who have been marvellous. For example, when I lead some sessions in Somerset one of the ladies on the team was nearly sixty. She wore a track suit and was ready for anything! At one point when things got particularly exciting, she was literally held upside down whilst demonstrating a handstand! This lady was a real inspiration to me and I wanted to take her round with me to show everyone that older people can be fun, can be pioneers and can lead children properly in a way that they can receive. What is more, she never wore a hat!

Another example that sticks out in my mind is an old lady in her eighties at a church near Bristol. Here I was leading some warm-up aerobic sessions at the start of the praise and worship (Rich's Worship Workout). I felt in a particularly silly mood and at one point ended up on my back with both legs kicking in the air! Imagine my surprise when looking round I saw this dear old lady actually lying on her back kicking her legs in the air! No one would have expected her to be doing this, yet she was putting herself out to be involved in what was happening and showing herself to be a fantastic leadership example. I felt like adopting her as my second grandma on the spot!

I am suspicious therefore, when healthy people in early middle age decide to opt out. It shows that there is something wrong with their attitude rather than with their body.

Making progress with the children
The mark of a true leader is that progress will be made in the lives of those we lead. If we are making no progress at all it raises some serious questions which we will have

to think through very carefully. Obviously it will not all be plain sailing. There will be disappointments as well as successes, frustrations as well as fulfilment. But through it all the underlying trend needs to be one of growth and progress.

Leaders sometimes talk down to children in a condescending way. In fact most Christian children have quite a sharp spiritual perception and are capable of receiving solids rather than the watered-down milk we more usually tend to give them. As leaders we need to ensure that we do not hold back their potential by our own lack of experience or understanding.

One very practical problem leaders face is the difficulty of finding suitable resources to run a programme every week which will help the children progress. It is easy for me to blast into a local situation like a whirlwind, see children released into, say, tongues and prophecy, and then say in effect to the leaders, "Now it's over to you!" as I head for home. How can it all be sustained on a regular basis?

Unfortunately there is no easy answer. To be honest I have not found any resource material that I am completely happy with. It all tends to be either too general, too traditional, too "middle-of-the-road" or too boring! We need something radical, something new. Until then much is going to depend on the gifting, personality and ingenuity of local children's leaders.

I suspect that lack of resources is only part of the problem – and probably a much smaller part than many realise. Even if a Super-Duper Mark 10 Megatronic Charismatic Resource did appear, I can imagine that in practice many children's sessions would still carry on with very little difference. This is because the printed material accounts for a relatively small percentage of what is actually communicated. Much more depends on the style of presentation and the emphasis individual leaders put on individual parts of the printed material. It would be possible for two different churches to be using the same new material and for one still to have a very traditional Sunday school whilst the other experiences all-singing-all-dancing child charismatic freedom! This suggests that it all has far more to do with the leader than with the material. It is certainly not enough to regurgitate the resource material slavishly without life and sparkle. Perhaps what we need is more leadership training rather than simply more resources.

Motivation

As has already been noted, some leaders do the job only to get out of something they think is even worse! It is a sad fact that some people are motivated to work with children not because they have a vision for progress in the children's lives but because it gives *them* a chance to escape from the main meeting!

To become a spiritual Houdini is simply not on. If the temperature of church life is too hot for us the answer does not lie in escaping, it lies in getting our lives sorted out so that we can be a part of and enjoy the meetings! Conversely, if the spiritual temperature is too cold we will soon run into trouble if we start ministering to our own groups out of sheer frustration.

Naturally our motivation should come out of love, care and concern for those we work with. The children will soon get to know whether we are genuinely interested in them or whether they are merely a convenient means to our own ends. Children need to be shown the qualities of love, discipline, sensitivity, power and authority if they are to be discipled according to the Kingdom principles of Jesus. These qualities cannot be properly conveyed unless we are genuinely interested in the children in their own right.

Knowing our calling to leadership

This is a crucially important issue. Unfortunately we tend to allow expediency to over-rule the need for calling. We should not wonder that we make little progress in the children's lives if we cannot trace our involvement to a calling from God.

Imagine the following situation. Some new Christians turn up at your church. After a few weeks someone approaches them and finds out that they want to join the church on a regular basis. A little while later a few tentative enquiries are made to find out what they can do in the church. They say, looking at the floor, blushing, and being quite humble about it, that they cannot do anything. Some "ministries" are suggested to them like sweeping the floor, putting the coffee urn on, doing some simple photocopying or – taking full responsibility for the entire children's ministry in the church!

This seems absurd but it is often not far from the truth. Children's ministry is put virtually on the same level as arranging the flowers, at least in some circles. What we fail to realise is that we are talking about a leadership position in the church. Children are people, just like adults. They need leadership just like adults. I do not know of any church that would recruit its adult leaders on a similar basis to our fictitious scenario. With adults' leaders we want to see evidence of gifting. We would like some experience. We need to see true anointing and (in the past especially) formal training. Certainly we need to see that the ministry has been growing and developing within a local church context and normally nowadays we would want to know which stream of church style the prospective leader represents.

When it comes to children's ministry all these high criteria are thrown out of the window. We will be happy to grab anyone we can! The fact that children's leaders are in a position to shape the most impressionable sector of the church would suggest that an anything-will-do attitude is probably more dangerous here than it would be in finding adults' leaders.

The problem of course is lack of people. We press anyone

into service almost at any price just to get a dirty job done. The carrot we often dangle is that the job is only temporary. "You will only have to fill in until we can get someone else" is the attitude. The only people who suffer from always having to receive from someone who would rather not be doing the job are the children. Surely they deserve better. Surely we must redress this gross and ugly imbalance.

It is so easy to be guilty of hypocrisy in all this. I find it interesting that the role of women has become such a controversial topic in the church. The controversy, of course, refers to the *leadership* role for women. We have always been happy for them to make our coffee, type our letters, clean our buildings and so on, but now men are getting worried about leadership. In particular they are becoming worried that their own safe domain might be threatened. Yet for generations we have been very happy for ladies to go abroad as missionaries and be involved in heavy-duty pioneering work in a full leadership capacity. Why is this? Simply because we as men did not want to get our hands dirty and go ourselves. We were happy to pack our ladies off abroad because we knew they could never threaten us from there. Men were never worried about the theology of it all then!

Similarly for generations we have been happy for thousands upon thousands of faithful ladies down through the years to be *fully responsible* for leading that whole sector of the church which comprises the children. Why? For the same reason. Men have not wanted to get their hands dirty in what is widely thought of as being a fringe, peripheral activity of the church. We let the ladies loose with children because it never threatened our own "proper" leadership positions. Again no one ever saw it as a theological issue.

The important point is to make sure that the right people do the job, rather than shovel it all off onto the ladies because it seems there is no one else to do it. I believe there is a great need to see men released into children's ministry. Real men who will be able to lead children into freedom and work together with our ladies to initiate a change in the character of children's ministry in this country.

God will, I believe, give us the resources we need to do the job he has called us to do. In a church context looking at children's ministry we should not be limited by what we see around us. If we do not have proper musicians or leaders, we need to pray them in! Certainly we need to pray as a church and find out what God has to say. We tend to run into trouble when we try to do the best we can in our own strength with only the people, equipment and resources we have now. We need to bring faith to bear on very real and practical issues. Let's get mighty preaching on issues like faith out of the safe environment of the pulpit and into the risky business of real life issues!

One final point needs to be made here. The view is often expressed that children's work is where people with a potential ministry cut their teeth. It is a sort of training ground, a place where mistakes can be made without it mattering. Then, of course, they have proved their ministry they can move on to greater things. We need to understand that there is nothing inferior or second class about children's ministry. And if the calling of God rests upon an individual to do it, there is no point trying hard to move out of it into something else.

The job of a leader
A leader's job is not so much to teach but to *be*. In summary the job will involve the following elements:

i) Getting the foundations right in our own lives first. This means we may have to receive help, ministry and encouragement ourselves whenever necessary.

ii) Understanding, relating to and communicating effectively with the children.

iii) Seeing children built into the ordinary programme of the church, rather than being a separate hived-off entity.

iv) Developing a strategy for progress.

v) Training and motivating others.

vi) Being flexible enough to adapt quickly and positively to change.

Contrary to popular belief, children's leadership is a high calling. It should be approached in the same way as any adult ministry. It is not a peripheral job, rather it is one of the most strategic ministries in the church. Praise God for the thousands of unsung heroes who have given their whole lives, often completely unnoticed, for the sake of training up children in the Kingdom of God!

Chapter 15

Church Structure

New wine requires new wineskins. If we try to put new wine into old skins it is only a matter of time before there is a horrible mess on the floor! There is abundant new wine available for our children. It is part of our responsibility to provide the right environment – the new skin – to hold it.

If we are to take seriously the call to see renewal, restoration and revival reaching down to our children, the question to ask is whether the time is now right to look at our church structure to see if any adjustments are required. This, of course, is primarily a matter for leaders and it is hoped that leaders will grasp the nettle firmly and look at this most important issue.

When our little boy, Sam, was a tiny baby both Lynda and I were very inexperienced. We had never been parents before! When I drove out of the Tavistock maternity home with Lynda and a pink bundle of flesh called Sam I suddenly realised that we were now all on our own. From now on he was our responsibility.

It would have been ridiculous, unloving and plain irresponsible if we had been prepared to make no changes at all to our lifestyle. It would have been crazy if we had expected that Sam should fit in with us and that we could choose to be "free" and not feed him in the night, wash and change him and so on. If we had not been prepared to adapt to him at all, but expected him to adapt to us completely, it would have been disaster. Yet this is exactly what the church so often does.

A church sometimes asks, "Why do we not have any young people?" When a few basic reasons are suggested we do nothing about it and then wonder why we still have no young people. If we are going to attract them and if we are going to keep those we have already, we must consider changes in our style and approach. We must avoid getting locked into tradition that prevents us being flexible enough to change.

One church I visited in London invited me to run two meetings for children on the Sunday. The only problem was there were virtually no children! The Anniversary always takes place in June so they always have it. The fact that they no longer have any children to celebrate it with is apparently an unimportant side issue! I must admit that in some churches I have seen I am not surprised the children do not want to come – I am not sure I would want to, even as an adult!

A new approach for a new generation?
The whole issue of a new approach was thrown into sharp focus for me one Sunday morning when I was leading praise and worship in an adult meeting in a school building. My family was with me although Sam had been bundled off to the creche. As I was in full swing I noticed something out of the corner of my eye. Through a glass wall near to me I could see the creche in progress. I saw Sam with his nose pushed against the glass crying his eyes out reaching out for Daddy but not being able to get to me. My heart broke to see him there. I began to think and pray, "Lord, is this *really* what it's all about? Is this the way you want the church to be?"

I was in the "main" meeting. The children were somewhere else – no one was quite sure what they were doing but at least they were out of the way. We were getting on with the real business of worshipping God. Sam was crying for Dad.

It seems to me that if we are honest many in the church do not really want the children. They are often seen as a distraction, a nuisance and a hindrance to worship. Whilst we tolerate the children in the meetings for a short time because we think we ought to, the truth is that many people cannot get rid of the children into Sunday school quick enough!

The irony is that when the children arrive in Sunday school they are presented with a programme and activities with which, increasingly, not even the leaders are happy. Then the adults are left in the "main" meeting often wishing that progress could be made a little more quickly in the church. Older teens ,o to a stuffy old-fashioned Bible class and creche children cry for Mum and Dad. No one seems happy!

Is there a better way? What can be done? Who takes the initiative? What about opposition?

Form and content of children's sessions

Many churches have changed the old-fashioned term "Sunday school" because they think it sound outdated and traditional. Unfortunately they have put nothing better in its place. All that has been done is a cosmetic alteration to the name. People might hope that a new name means an up-to-date approach to children's ministry. The sad thing is that the style, ethos and content are exactly the same as before.

Children's ministry is much more to do with who we are and what we do than what we call it. Having said that, its title is not unimportant. Ask any marketing expert about product packaging and he will tell you how significant a name can be!

Even more questionable in my mind than the title Sunday School is Junior Church. This reinforces the old idea that children are part of the church of tomorrow, not part of the church of today. It implies that they are not part of the real church but only part of a toy church. The question so-called Junior Church presents is this: At what age do you as a

Christian become part of the "real" Church? The Bible only talks about one Church. The idea of a junior version does not appear anywhere in Scripture. If the real church is unacceptable to young people, we need to be changing that, not adding a further layer of confusion and mess!

I find it interesting that around the country there is a growing dissatisfaction about Sundays schools, mainly from those who lead them. There is a feeling that something new needs to take place. As has been mentioned already, resources are only a small part of the issue. It is not only a question of doing better things with our children. Whilst it may be important to see a new emphasis like praise and worship, using the gifts of the Holy Spirit, healing and so on in place of yoghurt pots, glue and toilet rolls, there is an additional underlying issue to consider as well. That is: how does our church structure help − or hinder − our ministry to children?

Two congregations?
Many denominational churches I have visited are, in effect, two churches within one. There are those who "go" in the morning and those who "go" in the evening. A relatively small percentage of both groups turn up to midweek activities.

If church is something we are rather than something we got to, and if church is based on relationship rather than ritual, how can we possibly condone this morning/evening arrangement? Our members need to decide whether they are with us or not. If they are with us they need to be committed. If they are not with us they should leave. As leaders we cannot allow our churches to be like this. It is not freedom to let people drift in and out as they please, it is spiritual anarchy! We will never build anything solid if we are nor even sure we know how many bricks we have got!

In particular we will never see the church built into a true family unless there is a real and genuine coming together. Our children will never become part of a church where the adults do not even meet together.

Radical pioneers

When that great pioneer Robert Raikes addressed himself to the issue of children in the Church, he was heralded as a radical in his generation. Thankfully God always gives us radicals to give the Church a good shake-up from time to time.

Robert Raikes saw that children could not read and write, and so could not read the Bible for themselves. He had a vision to teach children to read and write. This would put them in a position to receive spiritually and would make them better informed citizens into the bargain. The problem was that children from a young age had to work and so the only available time was on Sundays. His revolutionary idea was for a special school on a Sunday to be known as Sunday school. The Church was furious! This would take children away from Church, was a worldly influence and would be a backward move.

Now, two hundred years later, no self-respecting church is without its Sunday School. It is amazing how a concept so unacceptable in one generation can become the accepted norm in another. It is also amazing how something which starts as a blessing can very soon be the very thing that will hold us back! It is a little like eating manna – great when it is fresh, but there's nothing worse when it is past its sell-by date.

Nowadays of course children can read and write, thanks to fulltime education, so there is no need to have the "school" element. Despite this we continue with it because we are familiar with it. We are used to it. We have always done it this way. But in an age of new wine, we need to consider the wineskin.

A new model
The new model I am going to put forward is only one
suggestion. It has been used in my home church for many
years. It is not entirely without its problems. No system is.
It has, however, proved itself over the years. One cautionary
word of explanation: it is not possible to make any
thoroughgoing changes that will affect other areas of church
life if we are not prepared to make adjustments in those
other areas as well. Churches run into trouble when they
try to change one thing but ignore the knock-on effect on
something else.

1. Sunday morning and the whole family
Whenever we decide to do something as a family, we
generally try to do it together. If we decide on a picnic we
go together. If we go out for the day, we go together.
Whether it is going on holiday, watching TV, eating fish
and chips out of the paper, or whatever, we do it together.
Anything of a family nature is done by the whole family.

Yet on Sunday when people go to church very often the
first thing to happen is that they get sent off in different
directions. Creche, Sunday school, Bible class, "main"
meeting are all compulsory for the appropriate age group!
It is ironic that the ordinary family tries to do things together
yet the church family tries to do things separately.

I believe that Sunday morning is a time for the whole
family to worship God *together*. To me, there is nothing
particularly special about a Sunday. A church meeting could
be on any convenient day of the week. It just so happens
that Sunday is a day off for most people and is therefore
a convenient time. After all, the church is the people not
the building so whenever God's people meet together they
are "church". It is worth remembering in passing that for
the first four hundred years of the church's existence,
Sunday was a normal working day. The early Christians
decided to take the radical step of abandoning the Jewish

practice of meeting on the last day of the week, the sabbath, and instead did the very opposite. They met on the *first* day of the week, an ordinary working day. It was like us agreeing to abandon Sunday altogether and meeting instead on a Monday. I wonder how many of us would feel free to do that!

This is not an unimportant issue. If we see that every day is the Lord's, it immediately unlocks us from the religion of observing Sundays and opens up significant opportunities for better use of weekdays.

If a Sunday morning meeting is for the family it is not a time for the children only. An easy trap to fall into is to gear everything to children so that it becomes simply a Christian entertainment time for the children. This is not what it is all about. Conversely, one church represented at one of my recent seminars had an all-age meeting but did nothing to involve the children. They expected them to sit still and be quiet while everything was done in effect for adults.

Family worship means just that. A time for the whole family to worship together, learn together, fellowship together and enjoy themselves. Church is to be enjoyed not endured!

A typical family meeting in my home church would start with praise and worship. We use contemporary songs which reflect what God is saying at the moment, presented in a sensitive yet powerful and totally non-religious way by competent musicians. During this time anyone will be free to bring a Scripture, tongue, prophecy, picture and so on. This is by no means restricted to adults. Children are encouraged to contribute and it is rare that a week will go by without a child contributing in this way. Sometimes (but not always) there may be a drama, mime or other presentation. Then there will be a short children's talk followed by a couple of songs specifically for them and then sheets will be handed out. These are puzzle sheets

209

containing word searches, colourings, crosswords and so on all relating to the teaching the children have just received. Then comes the adult teaching on the same passage in order to bring a togetherness and all-age strategy to the teaching and thus be systematic. Depending on who is preaching some of the adults may be tempted to do a children's worksheet themselves!

One rule is sacrosanct. The preacher is allowed only fifteen minutes at the most, preferably ten. We have often talked about building a trap door at the front which will open during the sixteenth minute of a preacher's time – but perhaps that would be taking things a little far! The reason for a short word is simply this: Sunday morning is no longer seen as the only time for main programme teaching. It is primarily a time for the family to be together to worship God and to have fellowship with each other. Longer, more detailed teaching is something for another occasion during the week.

2. *Midweek meeting*
A number of different approaches for midweek meetings have been tried by different churches at different times. The one we have settled for is a main meeting together, normally on a Wednesday evening and involves both our congregations meeting together. This is supplemented by a system of pastoral care groups which meet occasionally on an ad hoc basis, for a meal, game, video, teach-in, walk or whatever.

Children are very much included in these midweek arrangements. They have their own weekly housegroup meeting in their own age groups, in place of Sunday school. Lynda is responsible for the 5–6s, there is a group for 7–10s and two for teenagers. The housegroup system works well, the only difference being that children's housegroups start at 6pm rather than 8pm. Once a month there is a joint Praise Party which consists of praise and worship, drama and teaching.

210

In all this there is one practical problem. Only one partner in a family will normally come to the adult meeting as the other is at home looking after the children. Although cassette tapes are made available, it is not the same. This is a perennial problem but one which can be overcome.

In my previous fellowship in Tavistock where I was responsible for the groups in Gunnislake, we introduced a new system. We saw the housegroup as an important priority in church life. We asked each couple to make their own babysitting arrangements with people outside the church on a proper, paid basis. No one was expected to do any favours, it was all paid for at the going rate. Then in the housegroup we took an offering so that everyone contributed and paid all the babysitters' fees. The system worked very well at housegroup level but may, of course, be more difficult to organise at church level, especially in a large church.

3. *No half measures*
Our meeting arrangements have affected our whole church life, not merely the Sunday morning meeting. It is a recipe for disaster to think that we can go over to all-age family celebration meetings on a Sunday morning and leave everything else untouched. It simply will not work. We cannot pick and choose, like ordering a Chinese takeaway. It is all or nothing.

There are a number of reasons why a move to all-age celebrations that leave everything else untouched will not work. Firstly the adults will miss out on teaching. If Sunday morning is not the time for main programme teaching and if the midweek meetings remain unchanged, this vital area will come under enormous pressure.

Secondly, the children will miss out, if there is not strategic age-specific teaching and ministry, and if nothing else is changed to accommodate it.

Thirdly, the existing meeting structure will no longer be

relevant. The meetings themselves will no longer achieve what they were set up to do. There will be tension and friction, which will lead to frustration and dissatisfaction.

It will not normally be possible simply to make a few minor adjustments in church life to overcome these problems. A much more thoroughgoing approach is needed. Something must be put in place to provide adult teaching. Something must be done for children. The midweek meetings will have to change to make this possible. There will need to be a high level of commitment to it – which will not suit "Sunday-only" Christians who see one meeting on a Sunday as sufficient to discharge their church-going duty!

4. A monthly family service?

I always advise church leaders to leave everything as it is unless they are prepared to go the whole way with family worship. A common compromise is the monthly family meeting. It will never work because it is a compromise. If we really believe in a family worship approach as the right one, we should go for it wholeheartedly. If we do not believe this we should not go for it at all. We cannot try to pick and choose in a vague attempt to get the best of both worlds and keep everyone happy. Leaders must decide. Either it is right for them or it is not. The monthly "family service" is often evidence of leaders' indecision. It can easily be a sop with which no one will be truly happy.

Leadership and opposition

The only people who are in a position to effect changes in the church are the leaders. For this reason I used to find it amazing that so often when I led seminars on children in the church all the leaders were missing! They presumably felt that it was okay for me to tell their children's leaders that we need radical change in the structure of the church and not be there themselves! But the real reason for leaders' absence was that they thought the issue of children to be a peripheral one. As busy people they thought this was one meeting they could opt out of. Now when I am invited I insist that someone from the church leadership is present.

However frustrated the rest of church may get, the fact remains that only the leaders are in a position to effect changes. It is therefore the leaders who must receive the vision for change. It is not possible to by-pass leadership and change things by back-door methods. The issue of releasing our children in the church is a matter for specific leadership decision.

Naturally when leaders take initiative there will inevitably be opposition. People will get upset. They will misunderstand what is happening. Some may criticise, moan and groan but at the end of the day there is a choice. If the people cannot submit to the leadership, they should move on to another church where they can. Leaders should be supported and encouraged, they need it just like everyone else! But leaders must lead, it is their job. We cannot duck out of important issues, even controversial ones. Important issues are there to be faced up to, not to run away from. A leader who takes the line of least resistance trying to please everyone will end up going nowhere and pleasing no one.

Chapter 16

Time for a Change

In all that has been said about children in the Kingdom of God, one thing is clear. The church cannot continue to lurch on from week to week, month to month and year to year without considering the issues which have been outlined in this book.

It is my belief that over the next ten years we will be hearing more and more about children in the church. This important issue is, I believe, very much on God's agenda for the church in the nineties. The church that pushes it all under the carpet and carries on exactly as before will miss out on a powerful move of the Spirit of God among children that others will experience.

Just as in the Welsh revival, not every church will be touched. Some chose to stay outside of what God was doing around them. They chose to stay in the comfort zone rather than on the danger line. History has a strange habit of repeating itself. Let us make sure that it is not our own churches that are cold and resistant. Let us support leaders as they explore a better way for the whole church family— one that will give our children value and significance.

What a tragedy it was when God sent prophets to Israel and they said "yes" but did nothing about it. What a tragedy it would be if we say "Amen" but then carry on as before. In the Kingdom of God we cannot afford the luxury of putting these things on the side of our plates for some future time. Now is the time to seek God, to act and to initiate change. Now is the time for a spiritual shake-up which will change the shape of our churches and put us at the cutting edge of all that God has for the Church in our generation.